MICROWAVE
COOKERY FOR 1 OR 2

by Pat Jester

Contents

ANOTHER BEST-SELLING VOLUME FROM HPBooks®
Publisher: Rick Bailey; Executive Editor: Randy Summerlin
Editorial Director: Elaine R. Woodard; Editor: Retha M. Davis
Art Director: Don Burton; Book Design & Assembly: Leslie Sinclair
Production Coordinator: Cindy Coatsworth; Typography: Michelle Carter
Director of Manufacturing: Anthony B. Narducci

Published by HPBooks, Inc.
P.O. Box 5367, Tucson, AZ 85703 602/888-2150
ISBN 0 89586-244-1
Library of Congress Catalog Card Number 86-81040
© 1986 HPBooks, Inc. Printed in the U.S.A.
1st Printing

Material From Microwave Cookbook
© 1982, 1983 HPBooks, Inc.

Cover Photo: Creamy Stuffed Manicotti, page 56

Microwave Cooking

This book will help you enjoy the full potential of the most revolutionary addition to today's kitchen—the microwave oven. Revised standard recipes and delicious new ones demonstrate the time-saving versatility of this exciting appliance.

Basic information and over 80 full-color how-to photographs will enable you to make the microwave oven work for you as never before. This incredible appliance is geared toward today's busy lifestyles.

ADVANTAGES OF MICROWAVE COOKING

Compared with conventional cooking, the greatest advantage of the microwave is fast cooking time for all but a few items. In turn, this saves energy and reduces heat output into your kitchen, a tremendous plus during the warmer months of the year. Fast cooking encourages maximum retention of nutrients and flavor in vegetables and other foods.

MICROWAVE COOKING TIMES

Unlike conventional cooking, the amount of food placed in a microwave has a definite effect on the amount of time needed to cook the food. Foods have to absorb microwave energy to cook. More food absorbing microwave energy means less microwave energy is available for each item. The same is true for the contents of a casserole. The amount in a large casserole takes longer to heat than the amount in a small casserole.

Another factor that affects total cooking time is the starting temperature of the actual food. Frozen vegetables take longer to cook than canned vegetables that start at room temperature. Food shapes also affect microwave cooking times. Microwave ovens cook food from the outside toward the inside. Therefore, thin foods cook faster than thick foods. The center of a dish heats more slowly than the edges. Select foods that are uniform in size and shape for more even microwave cooking. The composition of foods also affects microwave cooking times. Foods high in fat and sugar cook faster in the microwave.

MICROWAVE COOKING EQUIPMENT

There is a wide range of cooking equipment that can be used in a microwave oven. If you have specific questions, be sure to refer to your manufacturer's use and care guide. Generally, ovenproof glass, ceramic and pottery dishes without lead in the glaze, including clay pots, with no metallic trim or parts, oven cooking bags and frozen-food pouches can all be used for microwave cooking. Paper should be used only for short cooking times.

Plastics vary widely. Check the plastic cookware package description to find plastic utensils recommended for microwave cooking. Some will melt or distort, especially if used with foods high in fat or sugar. Baskets and wooden boards without any metal parts can be used in the microwave for brief reheating of foods, such as rolls. Many specially designed microwave utensils are available. They include browning skillets, plastic or ceramic meat-roasting racks, fluted tube dishes, muffin dishes and ring molds.

Although few, there are some items that should not be used in a microwave oven. Metal in any form should not be used unless the manufacturer of your oven states otherwise. This includes metal twist ties and dishes with decorative metal trim. There are two reasons for this. The most important is that it may cause *arcing*, which looks and sounds like lightning or sparks inside the oven.

The other reason for not using metal is that it reflects the microwaves away from itself rather than allowing them to pass through the material and cause the food to become hot. This shielding effect of metal can be used to advantage when cooking large items, such as roast meat or poultry. During the longer cooking time required for these items, some areas tend to cook faster than others. To prevent overbrowning, these areas can be shielded with small pieces of foil held in place with wooden picks. Never allow the foil to touch the oven walls.

If you are not sure if a dish is safe to use in the microwave, you can do a little test. Place 1 cup of cool water in the microwave beside the dish you are testing. Microwave at 100% (HIGH) for 1 minute. If the dish is warm, it is absorbing microwave energy and should not be used in the microwave.

Many people ask about browning foods in a microwave. Baked goods and meats that are cooked in a very short time do not have the browned appearance we are used to. If you feel that this is a disadvantage, here are some ways to overcome it. Glazes will enhance the appearance of poultry and meat. A browning skillet, called for in some recipes, is particularly recommended for cooking steak. You can also use one of the color-enhancing products now on the market. Frosting or a number of toppings using ingredients such as brown sugar, spices and nuts can be added to baked goods to increase their eye-appeal.

MICROWAVE POWER LEVELS

If you do not know the wattage level of your microwave oven, you can conduct another test to measure that power level. It is the same one used to determine the power levels for testing recipes in this book.

Fill a 4-cup glass measuring cup with 4 cups (32

ounces) of cool water. Record the temperature of the water. Place the water in the center of your microwave. Microwave at 100% (HIGH) for exactly 2 minutes. Immediately stir the water with the thermometer and record the temperature again. Subtract the starting temperature of the water from the heated temperature of the water. If you are using the Fahrenheit scale, multiply the answer by 19.5. If you are using the Celsius scale, multiply the answer by 35. This figure is the approximate power output or wattage for your microwave operating at 100% (HIGH).

Many manufacturers are also including wattage information in the use and care literature that comes with the microwave. You can call or write the consumer service department of the manufacturer for additional information. Another possibility is to contact the dealer who sold you the oven. It is still a good idea to test your own unit because they vary in wattage even when they come from the same manufacturer and are the same model. There is also the possibility that the manufacturer could have used a different test to determine wattage and might have a different result.

The actual wattage output will be affected by the power load in your community at different times of the day and year. Something to remember when putting a microwave in your kitchen is that no other appliance should be plugged into the same circuit as your microwave. If both appliances are operating at the same time, your wattage output could be drastically affected.

To figure out the wattage level at different settings, refer to the chart below. The variable-power settings are expressed as a percentage of 100% (HIGH). To find the wattage of a variable-power oven, multiply the HIGH wattage by the percent of HIGH power for that particular power level. If your microwave is operating at 647 watts at HIGH power, it will operate at 30% of this power or 194 watts when the variable-power control is set at MEDIUM LOW or 3.

Your microwave may have what are commonly known as *hot spots*. That means that one area has a greater concentration of microwave energy and consequently cooks food in that area more quickly. This is why it is so necessary to stir and rearrange foods or turn dishes during cooking. This action rotates the food through the hot spot and aids in even cooking. Some rearranging is also recommended for ovens with the carousel or rotating feature.

To determine where the hot spot is in your oven, watch which area of food in a large casserole starts to bubble first or which area of cheese on top of a casserole melts first. This is an indication of where the hot spot is.

Power levels can be changed while you are operating the microwave. If food is boiling too hard, reduce the power level so the food cooks more slowly. This is similar to using a burner on top of the range.

If you need to stir or check a food while it is in the microwave, the power will automatically shut off when you open the oven door. Check on the food, close the oven door and then restart the microwave. Or, if the food is done, turn the timer to OFF.

POWER LEVEL SETTINGS

Word Designation	Numerical Designation	Power Output at Setting	Percentage of HIGH Setting
HIGH	10	650 watts	100%
MEDIUM HIGH	7	455 watts	70%
MEDIUM	5	325 watts	50%
MEDIUM LOW	3	195 watts	30%
LOW	1	65 watts	10%

Arrange thickest portion toward outside— The outside edges cook more quickly. Placing drumsticks with the meaty portion toward the edge will promote more even cooking.

Pierce or prick—Pierce foods with membranes or tight skins, such as egg yolks, oysters, chicken livers and baked potatoes.

Give dish a half turn—If the skillet is given a half turn, the tomato in the bottom skillet will be in the same position as the tomato in the top skillet.

Give dish a quarter turn—If the dish is given a quarter turn, the pear in the bottom dish will be in the same position as the pear in the top dish.

Cover with paper towel—Use white paper towels to cover foods that might spatter and require only a loose cover.

Cover with waxed paper—Use waxed paper for a loose-fitting cover that allows steam to escape.

Cover with vented plastic wrap—Either fold back a corner as on the squash rings or cut a few small slits with a knife.

Cut a small slit in pouch—The red "X" marks a 1-inch slit that should be cut with a knife to vent frozen pouches.

Stir—Always stir outside edges toward center and center toward outside edge. The outside edges will cook first.

Rearrange—Move items from the center to the outside edge, and items at the edge to the center.

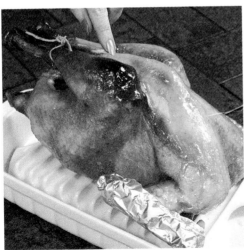

Shielding—Use small pieces of foil secured with wooden picks to cover areas that are over-browning or becoming warm during defrosting.

Cover—Use a casserole lid unless the recipe states to cover in some other manner. Or, cover with vented plastic wrap, above.

Eggnog Amandine

1 pint chilled eggnog (2 cups)
1/2 teaspoon freshly grated orange peel
1/4 teaspoon orange extract
1/4 cup amaretto

To garnish:
Whipped topping
Toasted slivered almonds
Freshly grated orange peel

1. In a deep 1-quart casserole with lid, combine eggnog, orange peel and orange extract; blend well. Cover and microwave at 100% (HIGH) 3 to 3-1/2 minutes, stirring every 1 minute, until heated through. Do not boil.
2. Stir in amaretto. Cover and microwave at 100% (HIGH) 30 to 45 seconds or until heated through.
3. Serve in mugs topped with whipped topping. Sprinkle with toasted almonds and fresh orange peel. Makes 2 servings.

Mulled Apple Cider

1 pint apple cider (2 cups)
1 cup carbonated apple wine or cider
1 tablespoon brown sugar
1/2 orange, cut in wedges
1 (3-inch) cinnamon stick
3 whole cloves
3 whole allspice
1/4 cup apple brandy

1. In a deep 1-1/2-quart casserole with lid, combine cider, wine, brown sugar and orange wedges; mix well.
2. Tie cinnamon stick, cloves and allspice in cheesecloth. Add to cider mixture. Cover and microwave at 100% (HIGH) 7 to 8 minutes or until boiling.
3. Remove spices; stir in brandy. Cover and microwave at 100% (HIGH) 1 to 1-1/2 minutes or until heated through. Makes 2 to 3 servings.

Honey Spiced Tea

3 cups water
3 tablespoons frozen lemonade concentrate, thawed
1/4 cup honey
1 (2-inch) cinnamon stick
2 mint sprigs
2 tea bags

To garnish:
3 or 4 lemon slices

1. In a deep 1-1/2-quart casserole with lid, combine water, lemonade concentrate and honey. Tie cinnamon stick and mint in cheesecloth. Add to lemonade mixture. Cover and microwave at 100% (HIGH) 6 to 7 minutes or until boiling. Stir to blend.
2. Cover and microwave at 30% (MEDIUM LOW) 5 minutes to blend flavors. Stir to blend.
3. Add tea bags. Cover and let stand 3 to 4 minutes to steep tea.
4. Remove spices and tea bags. Serve in mugs garnished with lemon slices. Makes 2 to 3 servings.

Special Coffees

Stir 1/2 jigger coffee-flavored liqueur and 1/2 jigger crème de cacao into each mug of room-temperature coffee. Reheat, then top with a scoop of coffee ice cream and a sprinkling of chocolate-shot candies.

Stir 1 jigger bourbon liqueur into each mug of room-temperature coffee. Reheat, then top with a swirl of whipped topping and a sprinkling of ground cinnamon.

Stir 1/2 jigger almond-flavored liqueur and 1/2 jigger orange-flavored liqueur into each mug of room-temperature coffee. Reheat, then top with a half slice of orange.

Eggnog Amandine

How to Prepare Make-Ahead Hot Chocolate

1/Measure 1/4 cup refrigerated chocolate mixture into mug. Microwave chocolate mixture to heat syrup. Gradually whisk milk into mug to blend with chocolate.

2/Microwave chocolate-milk mixture until heated through. Top with a marshmallow; microwave until marshmallow puffs.

Make-Ahead Hot Chocolate

1 (14-oz.) can sweetened condensed milk
1 (6-oz.) pkg. semisweet chocolate pieces (1 cup)

To serve:
1-1/2 qt. milk (6 cups)
6 to 8 large marshmallows

1. In a deep 3-quart casserole, combine condensed milk and chocolate pieces. Microwave at 100% (HIGH) 2 to 2-1/2 minutes, stirring every 1 minute, until pieces are melted; stir after 1 minute. Spoon into a refrigerator container; cover and refrigerate up to 1 week.
2. To serve, spoon 1/4 cup chocolate mixture into a 10-ounce mug. Microwave at 100% (HIGH) 20 to 30 seconds to heat syrup.
3. Gradually whisk 3/4 cup milk into mug, blending thoroughly. Microwave at 100% (HIGH) 1-1/2 minutes or until heated through. Stir well.
4. Top mug with a marshmallow. Microwave at 100% (HIGH) 20 to 30 seconds or until marshmallow puffs. Makes 6 to 8 servings.

Hot Toddies

4 tablespoons frozen lemonade concentrate
1-1/2 cups water
2 (6- to 8-inch) cinnamon sticks
4 tablespoons bourbon
1 lemon slice, halved

1. In each of 2 (10-oz.) mugs, combine 2 tablespoons frozen lemonade concentrate and 3/4 cup water. Add a cinnamon-stick stirrer. Microwave at 100% (HIGH) 4 to 4-1/2 minutes or until almost boiling.
2. Stir 2 tablespoons bourbon into each mug. Float a half slice of lemon on top. Microwave at 100% (HIGH) 45 to 60 seconds or until heated through. Makes 2 servings.

Herbed Tomato Cocktail Soup

2 cups tomato juice
1/4 medium onion, sliced
1 parsley sprig
1/2 celery stalk, cut up
1/2 small carrot, cut up
2 lemon slices
1/2 teaspoon dried leaf basil
2 peppercorns
1/2 small bay leaf
1/4 cup dry white wine

1. In a deep 1-quart casserole with lid, combine tomato juice, onion, parsley, celery, carrot, lemon slices, basil, peppercorns and bay leaf. Cover and microwave at 100% (HIGH) 4 to 5 minutes or until boiling.
2. Stir in wine. Cover and microwave at 30% (MEDIUM LOW) 6 to 7 minutes to blend flavors; stir once.
3. Strain soup and serve. Makes 2 servings.

Greek Lemon Soup

1 (14-1/2-oz.) can chicken broth
3 tablespoons Minute rice
1/4 teaspoon grated lemon peel
1 egg yolk
1 tablespoon lemon juice

1. In a deep 1-quart casserole with lid, combine broth, rice and lemon peel. Cover and microwave at 100% (HIGH) 7 to 9 minutes or until rice is tender.
2. In a small bowl, beat together egg yolk and lemon juice until frothy. Whisk in 1/2 cup hot broth mixture.
3. Add egg-yolk mixture to hot broth in casserole, whisking constantly. Microwave, uncovered, at 30% (MEDIUM LOW) 2 to 3 minutes or until mixture is heated through; whisk every 30 seconds. Do not boil. Makes 2 servings.

TV Mix Italiano

1 cup dry roasted mixed nuts with sesame sticks
1/2 (3-oz.) can chow mein noodles (1 cup)
1 cup corn-cereal squares
1 cup pretzel twists
2 tablespoons butter or margarine
1 tablespoon dry spaghetti-sauce mix
1 tablespoon grated Parmesan cheese
1/2 teaspoon mixed Italian herbs

1. In a 12" x 7" baking dish, toss together nuts, chow mein noodles, cereal squares and pretzels; set aside.
2. In a 1-cup glass measuring cup, combine butter or margarine and spaghetti-sauce mix. Microwave at 100% (HIGH) 30 seconds or until butter or margarine has melted. Mix well.
3. Pour hot mixture over nut mixture, tossing to coat evenly. Microwave at 30% (MEDIUM LOW) 4 minutes or until mixture is toasted and heated through; stir every 1 minute.
4. Sprinkle with cheese and herbs. Cool completely. Store in a tightly covered container. Makes 4 cups.

Nachos

6 tortilla chips
Canned diced green chilies to taste
1/3 cup shredded Cheddar cheese (1-1/2 oz.)

To garnish:
Taco-seasoning mix

1. Place tortilla chips in a circle on a paper-towel-lined 9-inch pie plate. Top each chip with a few diced green chilies.
2. Top with shredded cheese. Sprinkle cheese with taco-seasoning mix to taste. Microwave at 100% (HIGH) 25 to 30 seconds or until cheese melts; give plate a half turn after 15 seconds. Makes 6 chips.

How to Make Piquant Shrimp Dip

1/Stir in seafood cocktail sauce, shrimp and green pepper.

2/Spoon creamy shrimp mixture into a pie plate; microwave until warm. Garnish with parsley. Serve with assorted fresh vegetables.

Piquant Shrimp Dip

1 (3-oz.) pkg. cream cheese
1 teaspoon milk
1/2 teaspoon Worcestershire sauce
1 tablespoon chopped green onion
Dash freshly ground pepper
2 tablespoons bottled seafood cocktail sauce
1/2 (6-oz.) can tiny shrimp, rinsed, drained
2 tablespoons chopped green-bell pepper

To garnish:
Chopped parsley

1. Unwrap cream cheese and place in a 1-quart bowl. Microwave at 10% (LOW) 45 seconds or until softened.
2. Add milk, Worcestershire sauce, green onion and pepper. Beat with an electric mixer on medium speed until blended.
3. Stir in cocktail sauce, shrimp and green pepper.
4. Spoon into a 7-inch pie plate. Cover with vented plastic wrap. Microwave at 70% (MEDIUM HIGH) 2 to 2-1/2 minutes or until heated through; stir after 1 minute.
5. Garnish with parsley. Serve warm with fresh vegetables as dippers. Makes 3/4 cup.

Easy Bean Dip

1/2 (11-1/2-oz.) can condensed bean with bacon soup
1/2 (5-oz.) jar process cheese spread with bacon
1 tablespoon brown sugar
2 teaspoons Worcestershire sauce
1 teaspoon prepared mustard
1 teaspoon instant minced onion
1/8 teaspoon hot-pepper sauce
1/2 cup dairy sour cream

1. In a deep 1-quart casserole with lid, combine soup, cheese, brown sugar, Worcestershire sauce, mustard, onion and hot-pepper sauce. Cover and microwave at 100% (HIGH) 2-1/2 to 3 minutes or until cheese melts; stir every 1 minute.
2. Stir 1/2 cup bean mixture into sour cream. Stir sour-cream mixture into bean mixture in casserole. Cover and microwave at 30% (MEDIUM LOW) 1 minute or until heated through; stir after 30 seconds.
3. Serve hot with vegetable dippers and chips. Makes 1-1/3 cups.

Easy Bean Dip

How to Make Fruity Popcorn Treat

1/Drizzle honey into a mixture of sugar, butter or margarine, cinnamon and salt in a glass measuring cup. Microwave honey mixture until boiling.

2/Pour syrup mixture over popcorn, peanuts, sunflower seeds and coconut. Toss with 2 forks, coating all pieces with syrup. Microwave until warm. Add raisins and apricots or peaches.

Fruity Popcorn Treat

1 qt. popped popcorn
1/2 cup salted peanuts
1/2 cup shelled sunflower seeds
1/3 cup shredded coconut
1/4 cup sugar
2 tablespoons butter or margarine
1/2 teaspoon ground cinnamon
1/2 teaspoon salt
1/4 cup honey
1/2 cup golden raisins
1/2 cup chopped dried apricots or peaches

1. In a 12" x 7" baking dish, combine popcorn, peanuts, sunflower seeds and coconut. Toss to mix well; set aside.
2. In a 2-cup glass measuring cup, combine sugar, butter or margarine, cinnamon and salt. Drizzle honey into sugar mixture. Microwave at 100% (HIGH) 1 minute or until boiling; stir after 30 seconds.
3. Stir well. Microwave at 30% (MEDIUM LOW) 3 minutes; stir after 1-1/2 minutes.
4. Pour hot mixture over popcorn mixture. Toss with 2 forks, coating all pieces with syrup. Microwave at 30% (MEDIUM LOW) 3 minutes or until heated through; stir after 1-1/2 minutes.
5. Stir in raisins and apricots or peaches. Cool completely. Store in a tightly covered container. Makes 6 cups.

Popcorn

Trying to pop popcorn in the microwave without the proper equipment can be dangerous and even result in fire. Do not attempt to pop popcorn in your microwave unless you have a popcorn popper specifically designed for use in microwave ovens or are using the commercially prepared packets of popcorn for microwave use. You should not pop popcorn in a standard paper bag or in oil in a regular casserole.

1/Spoon tuna filling into small pita bread halves. Place on a napkin-lined plate. Microwave until warm.

2/Garnish tuna sandwiches with hard-cooked egg and avocado. Sprinkle with paprika.

Tuna Snack Sandwiches

1/2 (8-oz.) can juice-packed crushed pineapple
1 (3-1/2-oz.) can tuna, drained, flaked
1/2 cup shredded cabbage
1 tablespoon chopped green onion
1 tablespoon chopped pimento-stuffed green olives
2 tablespoons mayonnaise or salad dressing
Dash celery salt
Dash pepper
2 or 3 (4-inch) pita bread rounds, split crosswise, or 6 or 7 slices party rye bread or Melba toast

To garnish:
Chopped hard-cooked egg
Avocado slices
Paprika

1. Drain pineapple, reserving 2 teaspoons juice. In a medium bowl, combine pineapple, tuna, cabbage, green onion and olives.
2. In a small bowl, combine mayonnaise or salad dressing, reserved pineapple juice, celery salt and pepper.
3. Combine tuna mixture and mayonnaise mixture; toss lightly to mix well.
4. Spoon mixture into pita bread halves or spread on party rye bread or Melba toast.
5. Place on a napkin-lined 10-inch plate. Microwave at
1
th
6. Garnish with hard-cooked egg and avocado. Sprinkle with paprika. Makes 2 servings.

Soups & Sandwiches

New England Clam Chowder

4 bacon slices, cut up
1/4 cup chopped onion
1 cup frozen hash brown potatoes
2 tablespoons all-purpose flour
1/4 teaspoon salt
1 pint half and half (2 cups)
1 (6-1/2-oz.) can minced clams with liquid

To garnish:
Chopped parsley
Paprika

1. Place bacon in a deep 2-quart casserole with lid. Cover bacon with white paper towel. Microwave at 100% (HIGH) 4 to 5 minutes or until bacon is crisp. Drain, leaving 2 tablespoons drippings in casserole. Crumble bacon; set aside.
2. Stir onion and potatoes into reserved drippings. Cover with lid and microwave at 100% (HIGH) 5 minutes or until vegetables are tender. Stir in flour and salt until blended. Microwave at 100% (HIGH) 30 seconds.
3. Stir in half and half and clams with liquid. Microwave at 100% (HIGH) 7 to 8 minutes or until mixture begins to boil; stir after 3 minutes. Stir before serving. Garnish each serving with crumbled bacon. Sprinkle with parsley and paprika, if desired. Makes 2 servings.

Easy Onion Soup

1 (10-1/2-oz.) can condensed onion soup
3/4 soup can water
1/4 soup can dry white wine
1 teaspoon Worcestershire sauce
1/2 teaspoon sugar
2 plain rusks
1/2 cup shredded mozzarella cheese (2 oz.)

1. In a deep 1-1/2-quart casserole with lid, stir together soup, water, wine, Worcestershire sauce and sugar. Cover and microwave at 100% (HIGH) 4 to 5 minutes or until boiling; stir after 2 minutes.
2. Ladle into 2 soup bowls. Top with rusks. Sprinkle with mozzarella cheese. Microwave at 100% (HIGH) 2 minutes or until cheese is melted. Makes 2 servings.

Home-Style Chicken-Noodle Soup

1-1/2 lbs. broiler-fryer chicken pieces
2 cups water
1/4 cup chopped onion
1/4 cup chopped celery
1/4 cup chopped carrot
1-1/2 teaspoons chicken bouillon granules
1 teaspoon poultry seasoning
8 peppercorns
1/2 cup medium noodles
1/2 teaspoon salt

1. In a deep 3-quart casserole with lid, arrange chicken with meaty pieces to outer edges. Add water; stir in onion, celery, carrot, chicken bouillon granules and poultry seasoning. Tie peppercorns in cheesecloth; add to soup.
2. Cover and microwave at 100% (HIGH) 10 minutes or until beginning to boil. Microwave at 30% (MEDIUM LOW) 10 minutes. Rearrange chicken pieces. Stir in noodles, making sure noodles are under broth.
3. Cover and microwave at 30% (MEDIUM LOW) 15 minutes or until noodles and chicken are tender; stir and give dish a half turn every 5 minutes. Remove chicken pieces and peppercorns from soup. Skim fat from soup.
4. Remove bones and skin from chicken; discard bones and skin. Cut up chicken; return 3/4 cup chicken to soup. Refrigerate remaining chicken for another use. Microwave soup at 100% (HIGH) 4 to 5 minutes or until heated through. Makes 2 servings.

Home-Style Chicken-Noodle Soup

How to Make Lamb & Lentil Soup

1/Lamb shanks are the lower part of the leg of lamb and make a delicious broth. Add chopped celery, onion and carrot to shanks; then add lentils and water.

2/Serve steaming soup in bowls topped with zucchini, sliced mushrooms, mint or parsley and a dollop of yogurt.

Lamb & Lentil Soup

4 oz. dried lentils (2/3 cup)
1 (1-lb.) lamb shank
1/4 cup chopped celery
1/4 cup chopped onion
1/4 cup chopped carrot
3 to 3-1/2 cups water
2 teaspoons Worcestershire sauce
1 small bay leaf
1/2 teaspoon salt
1/4 teaspoon garlic salt
1/2 teaspoon dried leaf marjoram
1/2 teaspoon dried leaf thyme
1/4 teaspoon white pepper

To garnish:
Sliced fresh mushrooms
Chopped zucchini
Chopped mint or parsley
Plain yogurt

1. Rinse and drain lentils. In a deep 3-quart casserole with lid, combine lamb shank, celery, onion, carrot, lentils and water. Stir in Worcestershire sauce, bay leaf, salt, garlic salt, marjoram, thyme and white pepper.
2. Cover and microwave at 100% (HIGH) 12 to 14 minutes or until boiling. Stir well; cover. Microwave at 30% (MEDIUM LOW) 1 hour or until lamb and lentils are tender; stir occasionally. Turn lamb shank over after 30 minutes.
3. When tender, remove lamb shank from soup. Cut meat from bone; return meat to soup. Discard bone. Skim off excess fat; cover. Microwave at 100% (HIGH) 2 to 3 minutes or until heated through. Remove bay leaf. Serve topped with mushrooms, zucchini, mint or parsley and yogurt. Makes 2 servings.

Tips for Soup

Individual servings of soup can be heated quickly in mugs or bowls. Big batches of soup made on top of the range can be frozen in individual portions, then reheated in the microwave. And there's an added bonus—they don't stick to the dish!

Soups should be at least 170F (75C) before serving. Be sure to stir soups before serving to help equalize the temperature throughout. Remember that soups bubble around the edges long before the center is hot.

How to Make Oyster Stew

1/Microwave oysters briefly in hot butter and onion mixture until oysters are puffed and a few edges start to curl. Stir in warm milk mixture.

2/After milk and oysters are heated at 30% (MEDIUM LOW), add dollops of whipped cream; reheat briefly before serving.

Oyster Stew

1/2 pint fresh shucked oysters (12 oysters)
1-1/2 cups milk
2 tablespoons butter or margarine
2 tablespoons chopped onion
1/4 teaspoon celery salt
1/4 teaspoon dried leaf thyme, crushed
1/8 teaspoon dry mustard
Dash freshly ground pepper
Dash hot-pepper sauce
1/2 cup whipping cream, whipped

1. Drain oysters, reserving 1/4 cup liquor. Place milk and reserved oyster liquor in a 2-cup glass measuring cup. Microwave at 100% (HIGH) 3 minutes or until hot; do not boil. Set aside.
2. Place butter or margarine in a deep 1-quart casserole. Microwave at 100% (HIGH) 40 seconds or until melted. Stir in onion. Microwave at 100% (HIGH) 1 to 1-1/2 minutes or until onion is tender. Stir in celery salt, thyme, mustard and pepper until blended. Stir in oysters and hot-pepper sauce.
3. Microwave at 50% (MEDIUM) 1 to 1-1/2 minutes, stirring after 30 seconds. Cook until oysters are puffed and edges of a few oysters begin to curl. Do not overcook. Add warm milk mixture. Microwave at 30% (MEDIUM LOW) 5 to 6 minutes or until hot; stir after 2 minutes.
4. Top with whipped cream. Microwave at 30% (MEDIUM LOW) 2-1/2 to 3-1/2 minutes or until heated through; stir after 1 minute. Serve in warmed bowls. Makes 2 servings.

Grandmother's Bean Soup

4 oz. dried navy or pea beans (2/3 cup)
Water
1 lb. smoked ham hocks, cut in 2-inch pieces
1/4 cup chopped onion
1/4 cup chopped celery
2 teaspoons Worcestershire sauce
1 tablespoon chopped parsley

1. Rinse and drain beans. In a deep 3-quart casserole with lid, combine beans and 2 cups or more water. Cover and let stand overnight. Drain and rinse beans. Return to casserole.
2. Add ham hocks, onion, celery, 3 cups water and Worcestershire sauce. Cover and microwave at 100% (HIGH) 12 minutes or until boiling; stir well. Cover and microwave at 30% (MEDIUM LOW) 1-1/2 hours or until beans are tender; turn hocks over in liquid and stir every 30 minutes.
3. Remove hocks from soup. Cut meat from bone; return meat to soup. Discard bone. Skim off excess fat. Stir in parsley. Cover and microwave at 100% (HIGH) 5 minutes or until ham is heated through. Makes 2 to 3 servings.

Smoky Cheese Soup

2 tablespoons butter, margarine or bacon drippings
2 tablespoons all-purpose flour
1/2 teaspoon paprika
1/2 teaspoon dry mustard
1/2 (14-1/2-oz.) can chicken broth
1/2 cup milk
1 teaspoon Worcestershire sauce
1/2 (8-oz.) jar pasteurized process cheese spread
1/4 teaspoon liquid smoke

To garnish:
Crumbled bacon
Chopped parsley

---

1. Place butter, margarine or bacon drippings in a deep 1-quart casserole. Microwave at 100% (HIGH) 30 seconds or until melted. Stir in flour, paprika and dry mustard; mix well. Microwave at 100% (HIGH) 30 seconds.
2. Stir in chicken broth, milk and Worcestershire sauce. Microwave at 100% (HIGH) 4 minutes or until mixture thickens and bubbles; stir every 1 minute.
3. Stir in cheese and liquid smoke. Microwave at 30% (MEDIUM LOW) 5 to 6 minutes or until heated through. Stir before serving. Garnish with bacon and parsley. Makes 1 to 2 servings.

Grilled Reuben Sandwiches

4 slices rye bread
2 tablespoons butter or margarine, softened
2/3 cup sauerkraut, drained, chopped
6 oz. sliced corned beef
2 tablespoons bottled Thousand Island dressing
2 Swiss-cheese slices (2 oz.)

---

1. Spread both sides of bread with butter or margarine. Place half the slices on a plate. Rinse sauerkraut, if desired. Layer in order on bread slices: corned beef, sauerkraut, Thousand Island dressing, cheese and remaining bread slices.
2. Preheat browning skillet, uncovered, at 100% (HIGH) 4 minutes. Quickly place sandwiches in browning skillet. Microwave at 100% (HIGH) 30 seconds. Turn sandwiches over. Microwave at 100% (HIGH) 30 to 60 seconds or until toasted and centers are hot. Makes 2 servings.

California Corn Bisque

1 (7-oz.) can whole-kernel corn, drained
1/2 (14-1/2-oz.) can chicken broth
2 tablespoons butter or margarine
2 tablespoons chopped green onion
2 tablespoons all-purpose flour
1/4 teaspoon celery salt
Dash pepper
3/4 cup milk
1 tablespoon chopped pimento
1 tablespoon diced green chilies
1/2 cup shredded Monterey Jack cheese (2 oz.)

To garnish:
2 avocado slices
2 thin tomato wedges
Chopped parsley

---

1. In a blender or food processor, combine corn and 1/2 cup chicken broth. Cover and process until smooth. Add remaining broth; set aside.
2. Place butter or margarine in a deep 1-1/2-quart casserole. Microwave at 100% (HIGH) 30 seconds or until melted. Add green onion. Microwave at 100% (HIGH) 1 to 1-1/2 minutes or until tender.
3. Stir in flour, celery salt and pepper. Microwave at 100% (HIGH) 30 seconds. Whisk in corn mixture and milk. Microwave at 100% (HIGH) 6 to 8 minutes or until thickened and bubbly; stir every 2 minutes.
4. Stir in pimento and chilies. Stir in cheese until melted. Microwave at 100% (HIGH) 2 to 3 minutes or until heated through. Ladle soup into bowls. Top with avocado slices and tomato wedges. Sprinkle with parsley. Makes 2 servings.

California Corn Bisque

Creamy Fruited Bagels

1/2 (3-oz.) pkg. cream cheese
3 tablespoons drained crushed pineapple
1 tablespoon chopped green-bell pepper
1 tablespoon chopped pecans
1 teaspoon minced green onion
2 bagels, split

1. Unwrap cream cheese; place in a medium bowl. Microwave at 10% (LOW) 45 seconds or until softened. Add crushed pineapple, green pepper, pecans and green onion; mix well.
2. Spread on cut surfaces of bagels. Place on a paper-towel-lined dinner plate. Microwave at 100% (HIGH) 30 to 45 seconds or until cheese mixture is warmed. Makes 2 servings.

Vegetarian Pita Sandwiches

1/4 cup alfalfa sprouts
1/4 cup shredded carrot
1/4 cup chopped zucchini or cucumber
2 tablespoons shelled sunflower seeds
1 tablespoon creamy onion salad dressing
2 Cheddar-cheese slices
1 pita bread round, halved
2 brick-cheese slices

1. In a small bowl, stir together alfalfa sprouts, carrot, zucchini or cucumber, sunflower seeds and onion dressing.
2. Place Cheddar-cheese slices inside pita-bread pockets, resting on flatter side of pocket. Top with sprout mixture, then brick-cheese slices. Place sandwiches on a paper-towel-lined plate. Microwave at 100% (HIGH) 45 to 60 seconds or until cheese begins to melt. Makes 2 servings.

Hawaiian Ham & Swiss Sandwiches

2 slices rye toast
2 ham slices
2 pineapple slices, drained
1/2 cup shredded Swiss cheese (2 oz.)
2 teaspoons chopped parsley
2 tablespoons mayonnaise or salad dressing
1/2 teaspoon prepared mustard
1/2 teaspoon prepared horseradish
Paprika

1. Place toast in a paper-towel-lined 8-inch-square baking dish. Top each slice of toast with a ham slice, then a pineapple slice.
2. In a small bowl, stir together cheese, parsley, mayonnaise or salad dressing, mustard and horseradish. Spoon cheese mixture over pineapple. Sprinkle with paprika. Microwave at 100% (HIGH) 2 to 2-1/2 minutes or until cheese melts and sandwiches are warm. Makes 2 servings.

Deli Pita Sandwich

1 pita bread round, halved
2 thin ham slices
2 salami slices
2 Cheddar-cheese slices
4 thin tomato slices
1/2 cup coleslaw, drained
6 avocado slices

1. In each pita-bread half, layer ham, salami, cheese and tomato. Top with a spoonful of coleslaw. Tuck in avocado slices. Place on a paper-towel-lined dinner plate. Microwave at 100% (HIGH) 2-1/2 to 3 minutes. Makes 1 to 2 servings.

Creamy Fruited Bagels

Meats

Old-Fashioned Chili

8 oz. lean ground beef
1/4 cup chopped onion
2 tablespoons chopped green-bell pepper
1 (8-oz.) can tomatoes, cut up
1/2 (8-oz.) can tomato sauce
1/2 teaspoon dried leaf oregano
1 small bay leaf
1/2 teaspoon chili powder
1/4 teaspoon salt
1 (8-oz.) can kidney beans, drained, rinsed
To garnish:
Shredded Cheddar cheese

1. Crumble meat into a deep 1-1/2-quart casserole with lid. Add onion and green pepper. Cover with waxed paper. Microwave at 100% (HIGH) 3 minutes or until meat is browned; stir every 1 minute. Pour off juices.
2. Stir in tomatoes, tomato sauce, oregano, bay leaf, chili powder and salt. Gently fold in beans. Cover and microwave at 100% (HIGH) 4 minutes or until boiling.
3. Stir well. Cover and microwave at 30% (MEDIUM LOW) 15 to 18 minutes or until vegetables are tender and flavors blended, stirring after 8 minutes. Serve in bowls; garnish with cheese. Makes 2 servings.

Beef Cubed Steaks

1 tablespoon vegetable oil
2 (4- to 5-oz.) beef cubed steaks
2 teaspoons butter or margarine

1. Preheat a 10-inch browning skillet, uncovered, at 100% (HIGH) 6 minutes.
2. Add oil to hot skillet. Using hot pads, tilt skillet to coat evenly with oil. Quickly add steaks. Microwave at 100% (HIGH) 1 minute.
3. Pour off pan juices. Turn steaks. Top each steak with butter or margarine. Microwave at 100% (HIGH) 30 seconds or until cooked to desired doneness. For medium steaks, meat should be pink when cut in center. Makes 2 servings.

Vegetable Burgers Deluxe

8 oz. lean ground beef
6 tablespoons cucumber-sour-cream dip
1/4 teaspoon onion salt
2 tablespoons peeled, seeded chopped cucumber
2 teaspoons chopped green onion
1/8 teaspoon celery seed
2 leaf-lettuce leaves
2 hamburger buns, split
2 tomato slices
2 green-bell-pepper rings

1. In a medium bowl, stir together ground beef, 2 tablespoons cucumber dip and onion salt. Shape into 2 (4-inch) patties, about 1/2 inch thick. Place in a 9-inch pie plate.
2. Cover with waxed paper. Microwave at 100% (HIGH) 1-1/2 minutes. Turn patties over. Give dish a half turn. Microwave at 30% (MEDIUM LOW) 3-1/2 minutes or until almost done. Burgers will still appear slightly pink in the center when done.
3. Timings are for medium-done burgers. For well-done burgers, increase cooking time at 30% (MEDIUM LOW) by a few seconds. Let stand, covered, 1 minute.
4. In a small bowl, stir together chopped cucumber, onion, celery seed and remaining 1/4 cup cucumber dip. Serve burgers on lettuce-lined buns. Top with tomato slices, green-pepper rings and a dollop of cucumber-dip mixture. Makes 2 servings.

Vegetable Burgers Deluxe

How to Make Cutlets Cordon Bleu

1/Spread beef cubed steaks with herbed, semi-soft natural cheese. Top with a ham slice and spread with more cheese. Top either broccoli or asparagus spears with Swiss cheese.

2/Fold over sides and secure with wooden picks. If not secured, bundles will open during cooking.

Cutlets Cordon Bleu

2 (4- to 5-oz.) beef cubed steaks
1/2 (4-oz.) container semi-soft natural cheese with
   garlic and herbs
2 thin fully cooked ham slices
6 asparagus or broccoli spears, cooked, drained
1/2 slice Swiss cheese, cut in half

1. Spread each cubed steak with some of the semi-soft cheese. Top each steak with a ham slice; spread with remaining semi-soft cheese.
2. Place 3 asparagus or broccoli spears in center of each ham-topped steak. Top with Swiss cheese.
3. Fold over sides and secure with wooden picks. Place steaks, seam-side up, in a 10" x 6" baking dish.
4. Cover with vented plastic wrap or lid. Microwave at 100% (HIGH) 2-1/2 minutes. Rearrange steaks. Cover and microwave at 30% (MEDIUM LOW) 3 to 4 minutes or until meat is done. Meat should be slightly pink when cut in center. Let stand, covered, 5 minutes. Makes 2 servings.

Chili Pot Roast

1 lb. beef chuck roast, about 1-3/4 inches thick
1/2 (10-3/4-oz.) can condensed tomato soup
1/2 soup can of beer
1 teaspoon beef bouillon granules
1 teaspoon dried leaf oregano, crushed
1/2 teaspoon chili powder
1/2 medium onion, sliced, separated in rings
1/2 medium green- or red-bell pepper, thinly sliced
1 small bay leaf
1/2 (15-oz.) can red beans, drained, rinsed

1. Trim off any large outside fat edges from roast; slash fat edges at 1-inch intervals. Pierce meat deeply on all sides with a large fork. Cut into 2 serving pieces. Place in a deep 2-quart casserole with lid; roast should lie flat.
2. In a medium bowl, combine soup, beer, bouillon granules, oregano and chili powder; whisk until well blended. Place onion, green pepper and bay leaf on roast. Pour soup mixture over meat, covering completely.
3. Cover and microwave at 100% (HIGH) 10 minutes. Microwave at 30% (MEDIUM LOW) 30 minutes.
4. Add beans. Turn roast over. Spoon vegetables over roast to cover it completely. Give casserole a half turn. Microwave at 30% (MEDIUM LOW) 30 minutes or until meat is tender. Meat is done when it can be easily pierced with a fork.
5. Turn roast over. Spoon vegetables over roast. Let stand, covered, 20 minutes. Serve pan juices with roast and vegetables. Makes 2 servings.

Chili Pot Roast

Meat Paprikash

1/4 cup chopped green onions
1/4 cup chopped celery
1 tablespoon butter or margarine
1 cup diced cooked beef or lamb
1 (8-oz.) can red beans or kidney beans, drained, rinsed
1 (8-oz.) can tomatoes, cut up
1/2 teaspoon paprika
2 teaspoons all-purpose flour
1/2 cup dairy sour cream
Hot cooked noodles

To garnish:
Chopped parsley

---

1. In a 1-quart casserole with lid, combine green onions, celery and butter or margarine. Microwave at 100% (HIGH) 2 to 3 minutes or until tender.
2. Stir in meat, beans, tomatoes and paprika. Cover and microwave at 100% (HIGH) 4 minutes or until boiling around edges; stir well. Cover and microwave at 30% (MEDIUM LOW) 6 to 8 minutes or until heated through.
3. In a small bowl, stir flour into sour cream until blended. Stir 1/4 to 1/2 cup hot casserole liquid into sour-cream mixture; stir mixture into casserole. Microwave at 30% (MEDIUM LOW) 2 minutes or until heated through; stir after 1 minute. Do not boil. Serve over hot noodles. Garnish with parsley. Makes 2 servings.

Tips for Meat

You can save time by cooking most meats in the microwave. In addition, there are fewer preparation dishes and no baked-on mess to clean up. A few meats, such as pot roast, take almost as long to cook in the microwave as they would conventionally. In addition, these meats usually require more attention from the cook when the microwave is used. Unless the microwave is the only cooking device available, it may be less trouble to cook these recipes conventionally.

Pizza Swiss Steak

8 oz. beef or veal round steak, 1/2 inch thick
4 oz. bulk pork sausage
1/2 cup sliced fresh mushrooms
1/4 cup chopped onion
1/2 teaspoon fennel seeds
3/4 cup bottled Italian cooking sauce
1 tablespoon all-purpose flour
2 tablespoons cold water
1/2 cup shredded mozzarella cheese (2 oz.)

---

1. For extra tenderness, ask the butcher to put steak through a meat tenderizer. Cut meat in 2 serving pieces; slash any fat edges of meat. With a meat mallet, pound meat on both sides until it is 1/4 inch thick; set aside.
2. In a deep 1-quart casserole with lid, combine sausage, mushrooms and onion. Microwave at 100% (HIGH) 3 minutes; stir every 1 minute. Drain well.
3. Stir in fennel seeds and Italian cooking sauce. Add steak pieces to sauce in same casserole, making sure all meat is covered by sauce.
4. Cover and microwave at 100% (HIGH) 5 minutes. Microwave at 30% (MEDIUM LOW) 10 minutes. Remove steak from casserole; skim off fat from sauce.
5. In a screw-top jar, shake together flour and cold water; stir into sauce in casserole. Microwave at 100% (HIGH) 3 minutes or until thickened and bubbly; stir every 1 minute.
6. Add steaks to sauce, making sure meat is covered by sauce. Cover and microwave at 30% (MEDIUM LOW) 10 minutes or until meat is easily pierced with a fork. Sprinkle with cheese. Let stand, covered, 10 minutes. Makes 2 servings.

1/Cut meat in serving-size pieces. Slash fat edges of meat. Coat meat on both sides with seasoned flour. Pound both sides with a meat mallet until 1/4 inch thick. Pounding makes meat more tender.

2/Place meat in deep casserole. Sprinkle meat with chopped onion, green pepper and bouillon granules. Cut up tomatoes; stir Worcestershire sauce into tomatoes before pouring over meat. Make sure meat is covered with tomato mixture.

3/Partway through cooking time, stir rice into casserole until moistened. Rice not mixed with sauce will remain hard after cooking.

4/Let casserole stand, covered, 10 minutes after cooking. This makes the meat more tender and rice more fluffy. Serve rice mixture over steak.

Swiss Steak & Rice

8 oz. beef round steak, 1/2 inch thick
1 tablespoon all-purpose flour
1/2 teaspoon dry mustard
2 tablespoons chopped onion
1 tablespoon chopped green-bell pepper
1 teaspoon beef bouillon granules
1 (8-oz.) can tomatoes, cut up
1 teaspoon Worcestershire sauce
1/3 cup Minute rice

1. For extra tenderness, ask the butcher to put steak through a meat tenderizer. Cut meat in 2 serving pieces; slash any fat edges of meat.

2. In a small bowl, mix flour and mustard; coat meat with flour mixture. With a meat mallet, pound meat on both sides until it is 1/4 inch thick.

3. Place meat in a deep 1-quart casserole with lid. Sprinkle with onion, green pepper and bouillon granules. Combine tomatoes and Worcestershire sauce. Pour over steak pieces, covering them completely.

4. Cover and microwave at 100% (HIGH) 5 minutes. Microwave at 30% (MEDIUM LOW) 15 minutes. Turn steak over and give dish a half turn.

5. Add rice; stir until moistened. Cover and microwave at 30% (MEDIUM LOW) 20 minutes or until meat is tender and rice is done. Meat is done when it can be easily pierced with a fork. Rice should be fully hydrated and tender. Let stand, covered, 10 minutes. Makes 2 servings.

Basic Stew

8 oz. beef chuck, or lamb, pork or veal shoulder
1/2 (12-oz.) can vegetable-tomato juice cocktail (3/4 cup)
1 cup beef broth
1 small bay leaf
2 teaspoons Worcestershire sauce
1/4 teaspoon dried leaf basil
1 small potato, cut up
2 small carrots, cut up
1 small onion, cut up
2 tablespoons all-purpose flour
1/4 cup cold water

1. Pierce meat deeply on all sides with a large fork. Cut into 1-inch cubes. In a deep 1-1/2-quart casserole with lid, combine meat, juice, broth, bay leaf, Worcestershire sauce and basil. Add vegetables; stir well, making sure meat is covered by liquid.
2. Cover and microwave at 100% (HIGH) 10 minutes. Microwave at 30% (MEDIUM LOW) 50 to 60 minutes or until meat and vegetables are tender; stir after 30 minutes. Meat is done when it can be easily pierced with a fork. Vegetables should be tender with pierced with a fork. Let stand, covered, 10 minutes.
3. In a screw-top jar, shake together flour and cold water. Stir into stew. Microwave, uncovered, at 100% (HIGH) 2 to 3 minutes or until thickened and bubbly; stir every 1 minute. Makes 2 servings.

Easy Beef & Noodles

8 oz. beef chuck
1 (10-1/2-oz.) can condensed onion soup
1/2 soup can water
3 tablespoons dry white wine
2 teaspoons Worcestershire sauce
1/2 (8-oz.) pkg. frozen noodles (1-1/2 cups)

1. Pierce meat deeply on all sides with a large fork. Cut into 1-inch cubes. In a deep 2-quart casserole with lid, combine meat, onion soup, water, wine and Worcestershire sauce; stir well, making sure meat is covered by liquid.
2. Cover and microwave at 100% (HIGH) 10 minutes. Microwave at 30% (MEDIUM LOW) 30 minutes.
3. Stir in frozen noodles. Cover and microwave at 30% (MEDIUM LOW) 30 minutes or until meat is tender; stir every 10 minutes. Meat is done when it can be easily pierced with a fork. Noodles should be fully hydrated and tender.
4. When meat is tender, stir mixture. Let stand, covered, 10 minutes. Makes 2 servings.

Glazed Ham & Squash

1 tablespoon butter or margarine
1/4 cup maple syrup
1/8 teaspoon ground cinnamon
1/8 teaspoon ground cloves
1 (1-1/2-lb.) acorn squash
8 oz. fully cooked center-cut ham 1 inch thick
1/4 cup orange juice
1 banana

To garnish:
Orange slices

1. Place butter or margarine in a small bowl. Microwave butter or margarine at 100% (HIGH) 30 seconds or until melted. Stir in syrup and spices; set aside.
2. Place whole squash in an 8-inch-square baking dish. Microwave at 100% (HIGH) 2 minutes.
3. Pierce squash in several places with a large fork; turn squash over. Microwave at 100% (HIGH) 5 to 6 minutes or until tender, turning squash after 2 to 3 minutes. Slice squash into 1/2-inch rings; discard seeds. Set squash aside.
4. Slash fat edges of ham at 1-inch intervals to prevent curling during cooking. Place ham in same baking dish. Pour orange juice over ham; cover with vented plastic wrap. Microwave at 100% (HIGH) 3 minutes.
5. Turn ham slice over. Microwave, covered, at 30% (MEDIUM LOW) 2 minutes. Pour off pan juices.
6. Peel banana; halve crosswise. Add squash rings and banana to baking dish. Drizzle with syrup mixture. Cover with vented plastic wrap. Microwave at 30% (MEDIUM LOW) 5 minutes, or until heated through. Garnish with orange slices. Makes 2 servings.

Glazed Ham & Squash

Fruit-Glazed Chop

1 (4- to 5-oz.) pork loin chop, 1/2 inch thick
1/2 cup white catawba grape juice
3 tablespoons cream sherry or marsala wine
1/8 teaspoon dry mustard
1/8 teaspoon ground ginger
1/4 (8-oz.) pkg. dried mixed fruit (about 1/2 cup)
2 teaspoons cornstarch
1 tablespoon cold water

1. Slash fat edges of chop; place chop, meaty-side out, in a deep 2-cup casserole with lid.
2. In a 2-cup measure, whisk together grape juice, sherry or marsala, mustard and ginger; pour over chop. Add dried fruit, pushing fruit down into liquid.
3. Cover and microwave at 30% (MEDIUM LOW) 8 to 9 minutes or until tender; give dish a half turn after 4 minutes. Let stand, covered, 5 minutes. Chop is done when it is no longer pink in the center.
4. Remove chop and fruit to a warm platter. Cover tightly with plastic wrap.
5. In a screw-top jar, shake together cornstarch and cold water. Stir into 1/2 cup pan juices. Microwave at 100% (HIGH) 1 to 1-1/2 minutes or until thickened and bubbly; stir every 30 seconds. Serve fruit sauce with chop. Makes 1 serving.

Saucy Scalloped Corn & Chops

1 tablespoon butter or margarine
1/4 cup chopped onion
2 tablespoons chopped green-bell pepper
1 (8-3/4-oz.) can cream-style corn
1 (8-3/4-oz.) can whole-kernel corn, drained
2 tablespoons chopped pimento
1/4 teaspoon dried leaf thyme, crushed
2 (5-oz.) fully cooked smoked pork chops, 1/2 inch thick

1. Place butter or margarine in a 10" x 6" baking dish. Microwave at 100% (HIGH) 1 minute or until melted.
2. Stir in onion and green pepper. Cover and microwave at 100% (HIGH) 3 minutes or until tender; stir after 1-1/2 minutes.
3. Stir in cream-style corn, whole-kernel corn, pimento and thyme. Cover with vented plastic wrap. Microwave at 100% (HIGH) 3 minutes. Stir corn mixture.
4. Slash fat edges of pork chops. Place on top of corn mixture. Cover and microwave at 100% (HIGH) 3 minutes. Give dish a half turn. Cover and microwave at 30% (MEDIUM LOW) 8 minutes or until heated through. Chops are done when they are hot in center. Makes 2 servings.

Creole Chops

2 (6-oz.) pork or lamb shoulder or blade chops (1/2 to 5/8 inch thick)
2 tablespoons all-purpose flour
1 teaspoon dry mustard
1/4 cup chopped onion
2 tablespoons chopped green-bell pepper
1-1/2 teaspoons beef bouillon granules
1 (16-oz.) can tomatoes, cut up
2 teaspoons Worcestershire sauce

1. Slash fat edges of meat; pierce chops deeply all over on both sides with a large fork.
2. In a small bowl, mix flour and mustard; coat meat with flour mixture. Place in a deep 2-quart casserole with lid. Top with onion, green pepper and bouillon granules.
3. Combine tomatoes and Worcestershire sauce; pour over chops. Cover and microwave at 100% (HIGH) 10 minutes. Microwave at 30% (MEDIUM LOW) 15 minutes.
4. Turn chops over. Spoon sauce over top of chops. Give dish a half turn. Microwave at 30% (MEDIUM LOW) 15 minutes or until chops are fork-tender and no longer pink in the center.
5. Let stand, covered, 10 minutes. Skim off excess fat. Makes 2 servings.

Fruit-Glazed Chops

How to Make Chili Dogs

1/Place hot dogs in buns on a paper-towel-lined plate. Paper towel absorbs moisture so buns won't get soggy. Cover hot dogs with another paper towel to prevent spattering.

2/Spoon warm chili mixture on each hot dog, then top with shredded cheese. Microwave just long enough to melt the cheese.

Chili Dogs

1/2 (7-1/2-oz.) can chili with beans
2 teaspoons ketchup
1/2 teaspoon Worcestershire sauce
1/8 teaspoon instant minced onion
1/8 teaspoon prepared mustard
2 smoked beef hot dogs
2 hot-dog buns, split
1/4 cup shredded process American cheese (1 oz.)

1. In a 2-cup bowl, stir together chili, ketchup, Worcestershire sauce, onion and mustard. Cover with vented plastic wrap. Microwave at 100% (HIGH) 1 minute.
2. Place a white paper towel on a luncheon plate. Place hot dogs in buns on plate. Top with a second paper towel.
3. Move chili to back corner of microwave oven. Place plate with hot dogs in microwave oven. Microwave chili and hot dogs at 100% (HIGH) 2 minutes or until heated through. Remove paper towels.
4. Spoon chili mixture onto hot dogs on serving plate. Top with cheese. Microwave at 100% (HIGH) 30 seconds or until cheese melts. Makes 1 to 2 servings.

Sweet & Sour Beef Ribs

1 (8-oz.) can juice-packed crushed pineapple
1-1/2 lb. beef short ribs, 2-1/2 inches long, 1/2 to 1 inch thick
1 small onion, sliced, separated in rings
1 (12-oz.) can unsweetened pineapple juice (1-1/2 cups)
3 tablespoons soy sauce
2 tablespoons honey
1/2 teaspoon ground ginger
1/8 teaspoon garlic powder

To garnish:
Pineapple rings, quartered

1. Drain pineapple, reserving juice; set pineapple aside. Cut thick ribs in half lengthwise. Pierce ribs all over with a large fork. Place ribs, bone-side up, in a deep 2-quart casserole with lid. Top with onion. Pour in pineapple juice and juice drained from fruit.
2. Cover and microwave at 100% (HIGH) 10 minutes. Microwave at 30% (MEDIUM LOW) 30 minutes.
3. Rearrange ribs, bringing ribs in center of casserole to outside edge. Be sure meaty sides of ribs are under liquid. Cover and microwave at 30% (MEDIUM LOW) 30 minutes or until fork-tender and no longer pink in the center.
4. Let stand, covered, 10 minutes. While ribs are standing, combine drained pineapple, soy sauce, honey, ginger and garlic powder in a small bowl.
5. Pour off pan juices from casserole and remove onions. Turn ribs meaty side up. Pour pineapple mixture over ribs. Cover and microwave at 30% (MEDIUM LOW) 7 minutes or until heated through. Garnish with quartered pineapple rings. Makes 2 servings.

How to Make Baked Barbecued Pork Ribs

1/Cut loin back ribs between every 2 ribs to make serving-size portions.

2/Arrange ribs, bone side down, in baking dish. Rub a mixture of dry mustard, celery seed and garlic powder over ribs.

3/Top ribs with onion rings and fresh lemon slices. Cover with plastic wrap and turn back a corner to vent. The onion and lemon provide moisture for ribs during cooking.

4/Push lemon and onion slices to center of dish when ribs are almost done. Pour barbecue sauce over ribs. Microwave to heat through.

Baked Barbecued Pork Ribs

1 lb. pork loin back ribs
1/2 teaspoon dry mustard
1/4 teaspoon celery seed
1/8 teaspoon garlic powder
1 small onion, thinly sliced, separated in rings
1/4 lemon, thinly sliced
2/3 cup bottled barbecue sauce

1. Cut ribs into 2-rib portions. Arrange, bone-side down, on a rack in a 12" x 7" baking dish. Overlap ribs slightly, if necessary.

2. In a small bowl, combine mustard, celery seed and garlic powder; rub over ribs. Arrange onion and lemon slices over ribs. Cover with vented plastic wrap. Microwave at 100% (HIGH) 5 minutes; give a half turn after 2-1/2 minutes.

3. Rearrange ribs. Microwave at 30% (MEDIUM LOW) 20 to 25 minutes or until tender; rearrange ribs after 15 minutes. Ribs are done when they are fork-tender and no longer pink in the center. Push onion and lemon slices to center of casserole.

4. Pour barbecue sauce over ribs. Cover with vented plastic wrap. Microwave at 30% (MEDIUM LOW) 10 minutes or until heated through. Let stand, covered, 10 minutes. Makes 1 to 2 servings.

Poultry, Eggs & Cheese

Roast Cornish Hens with Rosy Currant Glaze

2 (16- to 20-oz.) frozen Cornish hens, thawed
Rosy Currant Glaze:
1/2 cup red currant jelly
2 tablespoons crème de cassis
1/4 teaspoon ground allspice

1. Prepare Rosy Currant Glaze. Remove giblets from hens, if necessary. Twist wing tips behind backs. Tie legs together tightly with string. Make a small slit in back skin of each hen for release of steam.
2. Brush hens with glaze. Place hens, breast-side down, on a microwave rack in an 8-inch-square baking dish. Cover with a tent of greased waxed paper. Microwave at 100% (HIGH) 8 minutes.
3. Turn hens breast-side up and give each a half turn in baking dish. Brush with more basting sauce and give dish a half turn. Cover with tent of waxed paper.
4. Microwave at 100% (HIGH) 6 to 8 minutes; baste with glaze after 3 minutes. Hens are done when juices run clear when pierced with a fork between leg and thigh. A microwave meat thermometer inserted between leg and thigh should register 185F (85C). When done, brush Cornish hens with more glaze. Cover tightly with foil; let stand 3 to 5 minutes. Makes 2 servings.
Rosy Currant Glaze:
1. In a 1-cup glass measuring cup, combine jelly, crème de cassis and allspice. Microwave at 100% (HIGH) 1-1/2 to 2 minutes or until jelly melts; stir once.

Variation
Stuffed Cornish Hens: Lightly pack 1/2 cup stuffing of your choice into each hen. Skewer skin across body cavity with wooden picks to hold in stuffing. Microwave as above. Stuffed hens may need 1 to 2 minutes longer cooking time *per hen.* Cook until a microwave meat thermometer inserted in center of stuffing registers 165F (75C).

Crisp Pan-Fried Chicken

1-1/2 lb. broiler-fryer chicken pieces
1 egg
1 tablespoon water
1/2 (4.2-oz.) pkg. seasoned crumb coating for chicken
2 tablespoons vegetable oil

1. Preheat a 10-inch browning skillet, uncovered, at 100% (HIGH) 5 minutes. Make a small slit in skin on each chicken piece.
2. In a pie plate, whisk together egg and water. Dip chicken pieces in egg mixture, then in coating mix according to package directions.
3. Add oil to hot browning skillet. Using hot pads, tilt skillet to coat evenly with oil. Quickly add chicken pieces, skin-side down and with meaty portions toward outside of skillet. Microwave at 100% (HIGH) 4 minutes.
4. Turn chicken pieces over. Microwave at 100% (HIGH) 4 to 5 minutes or until tender when pierced with a fork and juices run clear. Check for doneness toward end of cooking time; remove any done pieces. Continue cooking remaining pieces until done. Makes 1 to 2 servings.

Poultry Doneness Test
Whole poultry is done when a microwave meat thermometer inserted between the leg and thigh registers 185F (85C). The temperature will rise very little, if any, during the standing time. For this reason, it is best to cook the poultry until it is done. As an additional test for doneness, the juices should run clear when whole poultry is cut between the leg and thigh, or when chicken or turkey pieces are pierced with a fork.

Roast Cornish Hens with Rosy Currant Glaze

How to Make Roast Turkey Hindquarter

1/Make a small slit in turkey skin; place skin-side down on a microwave rack. Brush with glaze; then cover loosely with a tent of greased waxed paper.

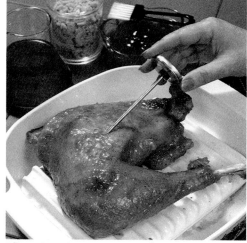

2/Insert a microwave meat thermometer at an angle into the thickest part. When turkey is done, thermometer should register 185F (85C).

Roast Turkey Hindquarter

1/4 cup Rosy Currant Glaze, page 36
1 (2-lb.) frozen turkey hindquarter, thawed

1. Prepare Rosy Currant Glaze. Make a small slit in skin for release of steam. Brush with glaze. Place turkey, skin-side down, on a microwave rack in a 12" x 7" baking dish. Cover with a tent of greased waxed paper. Microwave at 100% (HIGH) 4-1/2 minutes.
2. Turn skin-side up; give dish a half turn. Shield edges with small pieces of foil if these areas are browning faster than the rest of the hindquarter. Secure with wooden picks, if necessary. Cover with a tent of waxed paper. Microwave at 50% (MEDIUM) 28 to 30 minutes or until juices run clear when turkey is pierced with a fork. When done, a microwave meat thermometer should register 185F (85C) when inserted into thickest part. Brush with more glaze. Cover tightly with foil; let stand 5 minutes. Makes 2 servings.

Saucy Barbecued Drumsticks & Wings

1 tablespoon butter or margarine
4 (3-1/2- to 4-oz.) chicken drumsticks and/or wings
1/2 cup bottled barbecue sauce
2 thin lemon slices, halved
2 thin onion slices, separated in rings

1. Place butter or margarine in a round, 8-inch baking dish. Microwave at 100% (HIGH) 30 seconds or until melted.
2. Turn chicken pieces over in butter or margarine to coat. Arrange chicken in baking dish with meaty pieces toward outside of dish.
3. Spoon barbecue sauce over chicken, coating completely. Cover loosely with waxed paper. Microwave at 100% (HIGH) 5 minutes.
4. Top with lemon slices and onion rings. Spoon sauce over chicken. Cover with waxed paper. Microwave at 100% (HIGH) 4 to 5 minutes or until chicken is tender when pierced with a fork and juices run clear. Spoon sauce over chicken pieces before serving. Makes 2 servings.

How to Make Easy Oven Chicken

1/Shake excess milk or water off chicken pieces before placing in seasoned coating. Coat 1 or 2 pieces at a time.

2/Arrange pieces on a rack in baking dish. This baking dish has a built-in rack. Place meatiest portions toward outside of dish.

3/Chicken is done when juices run clear when pierced with a fork.

4/Dress up drumsticks with paper pants or make your own with colored paper and scissors. Garnish serving tray as desired.

Easy Oven Chicken

4 (4-oz.) chicken pieces, such as drumsticks, wings or thighs; or 2 (8-oz.) chicken-breast halves
Water or milk to moisten
1/2 (2-3/8-oz.) envelope seasoned coating mix for chicken

1. Make a small slit in skin on each chicken piece. Dip chicken pieces in milk or water; shake off excess liquid. Following package directions, shake chicken in coating mix.
2. Place chicken, skin-side up, on a microwave rack in a round, 8-inch baking dish. Arrange meaty portions toward outside of dish.
3. Microwave, uncovered, at 100% (HIGH) 10 to 12 minutes or until tender when pierced with a fork and juices run clear. Rearrange chicken pieces after 5 minutes. Check for doneness toward end of cooking time; remove any done pieces. Continue cooking remaining pieces until done. Makes 2 servings.

Chicken Cacciatore

1 tablespoon butter or margarine
1/2 medium onion, sliced, separated in rings
1 small garlic clove, minced
1/2 teaspoon dried leaf oregano
1-1/2 lbs. broiler-fryer chicken pieces
1 cup bottled Italian cooking sauce
Hot cooked spaghetti
Grated Parmesan cheese

1. In a round, 8-inch baking dish, combine butter or margarine, onion, garlic and oregano. Cover with vented plastic wrap. Microwave at 100% (HIGH) 3 minutes or until tender; stir after 1-1/2 minutes.
2. Turn chicken pieces over in butter or margarine mixture to coat. Arrange chicken, skin-side down, with meaty pieces toward outside of dish. Pour cooking sauce over chicken, coating completely. Cover with vented plastic wrap. Microwave at 100% (HIGH) 7 minutes.
3. Turn chicken skin-side up; spoon sauce over chicken. Cover with vented plastic wrap. Microwave at 100% (HIGH) 8 to 9 minutes or until tender when pierced with a fork and juices run clear.
4. Let stand, covered, 5 minutes. Serve chicken and sauce over spaghetti. Sprinkle with cheese. Makes 1 to 2 servings.

Chicken Salad Bake

1/4 cup pecan halves
1-1/2 cups diced cooked chicken
1/2 cup chopped celery
1/2 cup chopped fresh pears
2 tablespoons chopped green onion
1/3 cup mayonnaise or salad dressing
1 tablespoon lemon juice
1/2 cup shredded Cheddar cheese (2 oz.)
1/4 cup crushed sesame sticks

1. Spread pecans in a 9-inch pie plate. Microwave at 100% (HIGH) 2 to 3 minutes or until toasted; stir after 1 minute.
2. In a 9" x 5" loaf dish, combine chicken, celery, pears, pecans and green onion.
3. In a small bowl, combine mayonnaise and lemon juice; stir in cheese. Fold into chicken mixture. Cover with vented plastic wrap. Microwave at 100% (HIGH) 4 to 5 minutes or until heated through. Top with crushed sesame sticks. Makes 2 servings.

Chicken Tetrazzini

4 bacon slices
1/2 cup sliced fresh mushrooms
1/4 cup chopped onion
1/4 cup all-purpose flour
1/2 teaspoon salt
1/8 teaspoon white pepper
1 cup chicken broth
1 cup half and half
2 tablespoons dry sherry
5 oz. spaghetti, cooked, drained (2 cups cooked)
1-1/2 cups diced cooked chicken or turkey
1/4 cup grated Parmesan cheese (3/4 oz.)

To garnish:
Chopped parsley

1. Place bacon on a microwave rack in an 8-inch-square baking dish. Cover with white paper towel. Microwave at 100% (HIGH) 4 to 5 minutes or until crisp. Crumble bacon; set aside.
2. Remove rack from baking dish. Measure 1/4 cup bacon drippings into same baking dish. If necessary, add melted butter to make enough drippings. Add mushrooms and onion to bacon drippings. Microwave at 100% (HIGH) 3 minutes or until onion is tender; stir after 1-1/2 minutes.
3. Stir in flour, salt and pepper. Microwave at 100% (HIGH) 30 seconds. Stir in broth and half and half. Microwave at 100% (HIGH) 5 to 6 minutes or until thickened and bubbly; stir every 1 minute.
4. Blend in sherry. Stir in spaghetti, chicken or turkey, crumbled bacon and Parmesan cheese. Cover with vented plastic wrap. Microwave at 100% (HIGH) 8 to 9 minutes or until heated through; stir after 4 minutes. Stir before serving. Garnish with parsley. Makes 2 servings.

Chicken Tetrazzini

Creamy Stuffed Pasta Shells

3 oz. bulk pork sausage
2 tablespoons finely chopped green onion
1/2 cup finely diced, cooked chicken or turkey
1/2 (3-oz.) can chopped mushrooms, drained
1/4 cup coarsely crushed saltine-cracker crumbs
1 tablespoon chopped parsley
1 tablespoon dry white wine
1/4 teaspoon celery salt
8 conchiglioni (jumbo macaroni shells), cooked, drained, rinsed
1-3/4 cups Mornay Sauce, below

1. Crumble sausage into a 1-quart casserole. Add green onion. Microwave at 100% (HIGH) 1-1/2 to 2 minutes or until sausage is browned; stir after 1 minute. Pour off fat. Stir in chicken or turkey, mushrooms, crumbs, parsley, wine and celery salt; blend well.
2. Stuff 2 heaping tablespoons filling into each pasta shell. Place 4 stuffed shells, filling-side up, in each of 2 dishes. Pour Mornay Sauce over shells, coating pasta completely.
3. Cover with vented plastic wrap. Microwave at 100% (HIGH) 4 to 5 minutes or until heated through; give dishes a half turn after 2 minutes. Spoon sauce over pasta before serving. Sprinkle with cheese, parsley and paprika, if desired. Makes 2 servings.

Mornay Sauce

3 tablespoons butter or margarine
3 tablespoons all-purpose flour
1/8 teaspoon salt
3/4 cup chicken broth
3/4 cup milk
2 tablespoons grated Parmesan cheese

1. Place butter or margarine in a 1-quart glass measuring cup. Microwave at 100% (HIGH) 30 seconds or until melted. Stir in flour. Microwave at 100% (HIGH) 30 seconds.
2. Stir in salt, chicken broth, milk and Parmesan cheese; mix well. Microwave at 100% (HIGH) 5 minutes or until thickened and bubbly; stir every 1 minute. Mixture should be thick and smooth. Makes 1-3/4 cups.

Chicken Aloha Crepes

1-1/2 cups diced cooked chicken or turkey
1/2 (8-oz.) can unsweetened pineapple chunks, drained
1/4 cup chopped macadamia nuts
1/4 cup chopped celery
2 tablespoons chopped green onion
1/4 teaspoon celery salt
1/3 cup pineapple-flavored yogurt
1/3 cup mayonnaise or salad dressing
1 tablespoon dry white wine
1/2 teaspoon Dijon-style mustard
4 to 5 (6-inch) crepes

To garnish:
Toasted chopped macadamia nuts
Toasted coconut

1. In a large bowl, stir together chicken or turkey, pineapple, 1/4 cup macadamia nuts, celery, green onion and celery salt.
2. In a small bowl, stir together yogurt, mayonnaise or salad dressing, white wine and mustard. Reserve about 1/3 of yogurt mixture; set aside. Fold remaining yogurt mixture into chicken mixture.
3. Spoon about 1/2 cup chicken or turkey filling down center of each crepe; roll up. Place, seam-side up, in an 8-inch-square baking dish. Cover with vented plastic wrap. Microwave at 100% (HIGH) 4 to 5 minutes or until heated through; give dish a half turn after 2 minutes.
4. Top each crepe with a dollop of reserved yogurt mixture; then sprinkle with toasted macadamia nuts and coconut. Makes 1 to 2 servings.

Chicken Aloha Crepes

Canadian Bacon & Eggs

1 tablespoon butter or margarine
2 Canadian-bacon slices, 1/4 inch thick
2 eggs

1. Preheat a 10-inch microwave browning skillet, uncovered, at 100% (HIGH) 3 minutes.
2. Add butter or margarine; using hot pads, tilt skillet to coat evenly with butter or margarine. Quickly add meat at 1 side of skillet. Microwave, uncovered, at 100% (HIGH) 30 seconds.
3. Turn meat over. Using hot pads, tilt skillet to coat with drippings. Break eggs into a custard cup. Gently add eggs to other side of skillet. Prick yolks with a pin or wooden pick. Give skillet a half turn. Microwave, uncovered, at 100% (HIGH) 2 to 2-1/2 minutes or until eggs are done as desired. Let stand, covered, 1 minute. Makes 2 servings.

Tips on Eggs

Never microwave a whole egg in the shell. The egg will explode into more particles than you can imagine. Not only does this make a tremendous mess inside your microwave oven, it can be harmful if the egg explodes in your face.

Never reheat a whole hard-cooked egg in the microwave oven. Some hard-cooked eggs may explode if they are reheated whole. Always slice or quarter hard-cooked eggs before reheating.

Never microwave a poached, baked or fried egg without pricking the yolk. The egg yolk has a thin membrane over it. If this membrane is not pricked before microwaving, the yolk may explode.

Sausage Links & Eggs

1 tablespoon butter or margarine
4 fully cooked sausage links
2 eggs

1. Preheat a 10-inch microwave browning skillet, uncovered, at 100% (HIGH) 3 minutes.
2. Add butter or margarine; using hot pads, tilt skillet to coat evenly with butter or margarine. Quickly add meat at 1 side of skillet. Microwave, uncovered, at 100% (HIGH) 45 seconds.
3. Turn meat over. Using hot pads, tilt skillet to coat with drippings. Break eggs into a custard cup. Gently add eggs to other side of skillet. Prick yolks with a pin or wooden pick. Give skillet a half turn. Microwave, uncovered, at 100% (HIGH) 1-1/4 to 1-3/4 minutes or until eggs are done as desired. Let stand, covered, 1 minute. Makes 2 servings.

Pizza Egg Cups

4 salami slices, halved
1/4 cup pizza sauce
2 eggs
2 tablespoons shredded mozzarella cheese
1/4 teaspoon dried leaf Italian herbs

To garnish:
Fresh oregano or parsley

1. Place 3 half slices of salami around edge of each of 2 (6-ounce) custard cups, forming a scalloped edge at the top. Place another half slice on bottom of each cup.
2. Spoon half the pizza sauce into salami-lined cups. Gently slip 1 egg into each cup. Prick yolks with a pin or wooden pick. Top with remaining pizza sauce. Sprinkle with mozzarella cheese and herbs.
3. Cover each cup with vented plastic wrap. Microwave at 70% (MEDIUM HIGH) 3-1/2 to 4 minutes or until eggs are just set. Rearrange cups and give them a half turn after 2 minutes. Let stand, covered, 1 minute. Garnish with oregano or parsley. Makes 2 servings.

How to Make Pizza Egg Cups

1/Halve 2 salami slices for each custard cup. Overlap 3 half slices around edge of custard cup, then place other half on bottom of cup.

2/Add a spoonful of pizza sauce to each cup, then slip an egg into each cup. Prick membrane of egg yolk with a pin or wooden pick to prevent yolk from exploding during cooking.

3/Top each egg with another spoonful of pizza sauce, some shredded mozzarella cheese and a sprinkling of herbs. Cover each cup with vented plastic wrap.

4/Microwave eggs until yolks are just set. Eggs will finish cooking during standing time. Garnish each egg cup with oregano or parsley.

Deviled-Egg Tostada

1 cup shredded lettuce
2 tablespoons shredded carrot
2 tablespoons sliced green onion
2 tablespoons chopped zucchini
4 hard-cooked eggs
1-1/2 to 2 tablespoons mayonnaise or salad dressing
1 tablespoon canned diced green chilies
1/4 teaspoon celery salt
1 (8-oz.) jar taco sauce (1 cup)
2 (6-inch) corn tortillas

To garnish:
Shredded Cheddar cheese
Canned diced green chilies, if desired

---

1. In a bowl, toss together lettuce, carrot, green onion and zucchini; cover and refrigerate. Cut hard-cooked eggs in half lengthwise. Remove yolks and place in a small bowl; mash yolks. Stir in mayonnaise or salad dressing, 1 tablespoon green chilies and celery salt. Fill egg whites with yolk mixture; set aside.
2. Pour taco sauce into a 7-inch pie plate. Cover with vented plastic wrap. Microwave at 100% (HIGH) 1 to 1-1/2 minutes or until hot.
3. Arrange stuffed eggs in sauce. Cover with vented plastic wrap. Microwave at 70% (MEDIUM HIGH) 2 to 3 minutes or until heated through; give dish a half turn after 1 minute. Let stand, covered, 1 minute.
4. To serve, top tortillas with lettuce mixture. Arrange hot stuffed eggs and sauce on lettuce mixture. Sprinkle with shredded cheese and additional green chilies, if desired. Makes 2 servings.

Cheese Fondue

4 oz. process Swiss cheese slices, diced
4 oz. process Gruyère cheese, diced
1 tablespoon all-purpose flour
Dash garlic powder
Dash ground nutmeg
Dash fresh ground pepper
3/4 cup dry white wine
French-bread chunks
Kirsch

---

1. In a medium bowl, combine cheese, flour, garlic powder, nutmeg and pepper; toss to mix well.
2. Pour wine into a deep 1-quart casserole. Microwave at 100% (HIGH) 1-1/2 to 2 minutes or until bubbles start to appear; do not boil.
3. Stir in half the cheese mixture, mixing well. Microwave at 100% (HIGH) 1 minute or until almost melted. Stir in remaining cheese mixture. Microwave at 100% (HIGH) 1 to 1-1/2 minutes or until almost melted. Whisk until smooth.
4. Keep warm while serving. Dip chunks of French bread in kirsch, then in cheese mixture. If mixture becomes too thick, stir in a little more warmed wine. Makes 2 servings.

More Tips on Eggs

Most egg dishes cook well at 100% (HIGH). The exceptions are quiches and layered casseroles. They are cooked at a lower power so the centers will get done without overcooking the edges.

To determine if an egg dish in a large casserole is done, a knife inserted in the center should feel hot. Cooking casseroles is deceiving; the edges will bubble vigorously before the center is even warm. That is why bringing the edges of the casserole to the center by stirring promotes more even heating.

Egg and cheese dishes can be reheated in the microwave. Wedges of quiche and servings of casseroles reheat well in the microwave. Other items, such as scrambled eggs, cook so quickly in the microwave, it's best to start over. Reheating eggs tends to overcook and toughen them.

How to Make Denver Sandwich Pita-Style

1/Stir cooked portion of eggs around edges to center of dish and let uncooked portion flow to edge. When eggs are almost set, stir in yogurt. Yogurt will curdle if added too soon.

2/Split pita bread crosswise so each half forms a pocket. Spoon egg mixture into pita-bread halves. Top sandwiches with tomato, alfalfa sprouts and shredded cheese.

Denver Sandwich Pita-Style

1 tablespoon butter or margarine
1 tablespoon chopped onion
1 tablespoon chopped green-bell pepper
1 tablespoon chopped celery
2 eggs, slightly beaten
1/8 teaspoon salt
2 tablespoons plain yogurt
1 pita bread round, split crosswise
Chopped tomato
Alfalfa sprouts
Shredded Monterey Jack cheese

1. In a 9" x 5" loaf dish, combine butter or margarine, onion, green pepper and celery. Microwave, uncovered, at 100% (HIGH) 1-1/2 to 2 minutes or until vegetables are tender. Stir in eggs and salt. Cover with vented plastic wrap.
2. Microwave at 70% (MEDIUM HIGH) 1-1/2 to 2 minutes or until eggs are almost set; stir after 1 minute. Stir yogurt into egg mixture. Cover with plastic wrap. Microwave at 70% (MEDIUM HIGH) 30 to 45 seconds or until heated through.
3. Spoon egg mixture into pita bread. Top with tomato, alfalfa sprouts and Monterey Jack cheese. Makes 1 serving.

Cheesy Broccoli Stratas

1-1/2 cups herb-seasoned croutons
1 cup shredded process American cheese (4 oz.)
1 (10-oz.) pkg. frozen chopped broccoli, cooked, drained
2 tablespoons chopped pimento
2 tablespoons chopped green onion
1/4 cup bottled tartar sauce
1/2 teaspoon lemon juice
2 eggs, slightly beaten
1 (5-1/3-oz.) can evaporated milk

1. Butter 2 (2-cup) casseroles. Divide 3/4 cup croutons between casseroles. Top each casserole with 1/4 cup cheese.
2. In a medium bowl, combine broccoli, pimento and green onion. Fold in tartar sauce and lemon juice. Divide broccoli mixture between casseroles. Top with remaining croutons and cheese.
3. In a small bowl, whisk together eggs and evaporated milk; pour over croutons. Cover each casserole with plastic wrap. Refrigerate 2 to 24 hours.
4. To serve, cover with vented plastic wrap. Microwave at 50% (MEDIUM) 15 to 20 minutes or until set; give dishes a quarter turn every 5 minutes. Let stand, covered, 5 minutes. Makes 2 servings.

How to Make One-Dish Macaroni & Cheese

1/Microwave hot water, oil and salt until boiling, then sprinkle in macaroni. Oil helps prevent water from boiling over during cooking. Cover. Microwave at 30% (MEDIUM LOW) until macaroni is tender.

2/Drain hot macaroni. Stir in cheese spread, evaporated milk, chopped pimento and instant minced onion. Microwave briefly until heated through. Garnish with green-pepper rings or buttered cracker crumbs.

One-Dish Macaroni & Cheese

2 cups hot cooked macaroni, well-drained, below
1/2 (8-oz.) jar pasteurized process cheese spread
3 tablespoons evaporated milk
2 tablespoons chopped pimento
1/2 teaspoon instant minced onion
1/2 small green-bell pepper, sliced in rings

1. In a deep 2-quart casserole with lid, combine hot macaroni and cheese spread. Stir until cheese spread has melted. Stir in evaporated milk, pimento and onion.
2. Cover and microwave at 70% (MEDIUM HIGH) 3 minutes. Stir. Top with pepper rings.
3. Cover and microwave at 70% (MEDIUM HIGH) 3 minutes or until heated through. Makes 2 servings.

Macaroni

2 cups hot water
2 teaspoons vegetable oil
1/8 teaspoon salt
1 cup (3 to 3-1/2 oz.) macaroni

1. In a deep 2-quart casserole with lid, combine hot water, oil and salt. Cover and microwave at 100% (HIGH) 4 minutes or until boiling.
2. Add macaroni. Microwave at 30% (MEDIUM LOW) 13 to 15 minutes or until tender; stir after 6 minutes. Drain and rinse with hot water before serving. Makes 2 cups.

Macaroni & Cheese

2 tablespoons butter or margarine
2 tablespoons chopped green onion
4 teaspoons all-purpose flour
1/8 teaspoon celery salt
1/8 teaspoon freshly ground pepper
1 cup milk
4 oz. process American cheese slices, torn up
3/4 cup (3 oz.) macaroni, cooked, drained
2 tablespoons chopped pimento
1 tablespoon chopped parsley
3 tomato slices
3 green-bell-pepper rings
2 tablespoons grated Parmesan cheese

1. In a deep 1-quart casserole with lid, combine butter or margarine and green onion. Microwave, uncovered, at 100% (HIGH) 1 to 1-1/2 minutes or until onion is tender. Stir in flour, celery salt and pepper. Microwave at 100% (HIGH) 30 seconds.
2. Stir in milk. Microwave at 100% (HIGH) 3 to 3-1/2 minutes or until bubbly; stir every 1 minute. Stir in cheese; microwave at 100% (HIGH) 1 minute or until cheese melts; stir after 30 seconds.
3. Stir in macaroni and pimento. Cover and microwave at 100% (HIGH) 4 to 5 minutes or until heated through; stir after 2 minutes. Stir in parsley. Top with tomato slices and green-pepper rings. Sprinkle with Parmesan cheese. Cover and microwave at 100% (HIGH) 2 minutes or until tomato and pepper are heated through. Makes 2 servings.

Macaroni & Cheese

Fish & Seafood

Scallops Véronique

2 tablespoons butter or margarine
1/4 cup chopped shallots
2 tablespoons cornstarch
1/4 teaspoon ground mace
1-1/2 cups strained fish stock or chicken broth
1/4 cup dry white wine
1 tablespoon lemon juice
1 lb. scallops, poached
1 cup seedless green grapes, halved
Hot cooked white and wild rice

1. In a deep 2-quart casserole with lid, combine butter or margarine and shallots. Microwave at 100% (HIGH) 2 to 2-1/2 minutes or until shallots are tender. Stir in cornstarch and mace. Microwave at 100% (HIGH) 30 seconds.
2. Whisk in stock or broth and wine. Microwave at 100% (HIGH) 4 to 5 minutes or until thickened and bubbly; stir every 1 minute. Mixture should be thick and smooth. Stir in lemon juice; gently fold in scallops.
3. Cover and microwave at 100% (HIGH) 3 to 3-1/2 minutes or until heated through. Stir in grapes. Let stand, covered, 5 minutes. Serve over hot rice. Sprinkle with paprika. Makes 2 servings.

Fresh Shrimp in the Shell

1 (12-oz.) can beer
1 small bay leaf
1 teaspoon pickling spice
1 lb. fresh large shrimp in the shell, 16 to 20 shrimp per lb.

1. In a deep 2-quart casserole with lid, combine beer, bay leaf and pickling spice. Cover and microwave at 100% (HIGH) 3 to 4 minutes or until boiling.
2. Add shrimp. Microwave, uncovered, at 100% (HIGH) 4 to 5 minutes or until shrimp turn pink and are becoming opaque. Stir every 1 minute. Drain immediately.
3. Serve shrimp hot in the shell with melted butter. Or peel, devein and refrigerate shrimp. Serve as an appetizer with Seafood Cocktail Sauce, page 58, or use in salads or casseroles. Makes 2 servings.

Stuffed Lobster Tails

2 tablespoons butter or margarine
1/3 cup seasoned dry bread crumbs
2 tablespoons grated Parmesan cheese
1 tablespoon chopped parsley
2 (8-oz.) cooked lobster tails
1/4 cup sliced fresh mushrooms
2 tablespoons butter or margarine
1 tablespoon all-purpose flour
1/8 teaspoon salt
1/8 teaspoon paprika
3/4 cup half and half
1 tablespoon lemon juice
1/2 cup poached scallops or shrimp, halved

1. Place 2 tablespoons butter or margarine in a 2-cup bowl. Microwave at 100% (HIGH) 30 seconds or until melted. Stir in bread crumbs, Parmesan cheese and parsley; set aside.
2. Remove cooked meat from lobster tails. Cut meat in chunks and reserve shells intact; set aside.
3. In a 2-quart casserole, combine mushrooms and 2 tablespoons butter or margarine. Microwave at 100% (HIGH) 3 to 3-1/2 minutes or until tender. Stir in flour, salt and paprika. Microwave at 100% (HIGH) 30 seconds. Whisk in half and half. Microwave at 100% (HIGH) 2-1/2 to 3 minutes or until thickened and bubbly; stir every 1 minute. Mixture should be thick and smooth.
4. Stir in lemon juice, lobster meat and scallops or shrimp. Spoon about 1 cup filling into each lobster shell. Set shells in an 8-inch-square baking dish. Cover with vented plastic wrap. Microwave at 100% (HIGH) 4 to 4-1/2 minutes or until heated through. Makes 2 servings.

Scallops Véronique

Crumb-Coated Baked Fish

2 (4-oz.) fish fillets, about 1/4 inch thick
1/2 (2-oz.) pkg. seasoned coating mix for fish

1. Pour water into a pie plate. Dip fish fillets in water to moisten both sides; shake off excess liquid. Shake fish in coating mix.
2. Place fish, skin-side down, on a microwave rack in a 12" x 7" baking dish. Arrange fish with thicker portion toward outside of dish. Microwave, uncovered, at 100% (HIGH) 3-1/2 to 4 minutes or until center of fish is beginning to flake when tested with a fork; give dish a half turn after 2 minutes. Coating on fish will not be crisp. Makes 2 servings.

Fish in a Clay Pot

2 (6-oz.) fish steaks, 1 inch thick
Garlic salt to taste
2 tablespoons chopped fennel
2 tablespoons sliced leek
2 tablespoons chopped radish
Sorrel or spinach leaves
2 tablespoons butter or margarine
2 tablespoons dry white wine

1. Soak a 2-1/2-quart clay pot with lid in cold water 20 minutes or according to manufacturer's directions. Sprinkle fish steaks with garlic salt.
2. Combine fennel, leek and radish in bottom of clay pot. Place fish steaks over vegetables. Cover steaks with sorrel or spinach leaves.
3. Place butter or margarine in a custard cup. Microwave at 100% (HIGH) 30 seconds or until melted. Stir in white wine. Drizzle butter or margarine mixture over fish. Cover with clay-pot lid. Microwave at 100% (HIGH) 14 to 15 minutes or until center of fish is beginning to flake when tested with a fork. Give dish a half turn after 7 minutes. Serve fish with juices and vegetables. Makes 2 servings.

Slaw Fillet Roll-Ups

1/4 cup dairy sour cream
1/2 teaspoon prepared mustard
1/4 teaspoon prepared horseradish
1/8 teaspoon celery seed
2 (4-oz.) fish fillets, 1/4 inch thick
1/3 cup coleslaw, well-drained

1. In a 6-ounce custard cup, combine sour cream, mustard, horseradish and celery seed. Pat fillets dry with paper towels. Spread about 1 teaspoon sour-cream mixture on 1 side of each fillet. Set aside remaining sour-cream mixture.
2. Top each fillet with about 2 tablespoons coleslaw. Spread evenly on fillets. Roll up, jelly-roll style, starting at narrow end; secure with wooden picks.
3. Place fillet rolls on a microwave rack in a 9-inch pie plate. Cover with vented plastic wrap. Microwave at 100% (HIGH) 4-1/2 to 5 minutes or until center of fish is beginning to flake when tested with a fork. Give dish a half turn after 2 minutes. Let stand, covered, 5 minutes.
4. Microwave remaining sour-cream mixture at 50% (MEDIUM) 20 seconds. Spoon over fillets. Garnish with paprika and watercress, if desired. Makes 2 servings.

Hearty Tuna Casserole

1/3 (10-3/4-oz.) can condensed creamy
   chicken-mushroom soup
1 tablespoon milk
3 tablespoons chopped celery
1 tablespoon sliced green onion
1 (1-1/2-oz.) can shoestring potatoes
1 (3-1/2-oz.) can water-pack tuna, drained, flaked
3 tablespoons toasted whole almonds
1/3 cup shredded process American cheese (1-1/2 oz.)
2 teaspoons chopped parsley

1. In a 2-cup casserole, whisk together soup and milk. Stir in celery and green onion. Cover with vented plastic wrap. Microwave at 100% (HIGH) 2 minutes or until boiling; stir after 1 minute.
2. Fold in half the potatoes. Fold in tuna and almonds. Cover with vented plastic wrap. Microwave at 100% (HIGH) 2 minutes or until heated through; stir after 1 minute.
3. Top with remaining potatoes. Sprinkle with cheese and parsley. Microwave, uncovered, at 100% (HIGH) 1 minute or until cheese melts. Makes 1 to 2 servings.

How to Make Salmon Divan en Papillote

1/Butter squares of parchment paper. Layer cooked broccoli spears, pimento and poached salmon steaks in 1 corner of buttered side of paper. Spoon sauce over fish, then sprinkle with parsley and paprika.

2/Fold half of each paper square over fish, forming a triangle. Fold edges together twice to seal all the way around the triangle.

Salmon Divan en Papillote

1 (10-oz.) pkg. frozen broccoli spears, cooked, drained
2 tablespoons chopped pimento
2 (5-oz.) salmon steaks, poached
1 (10-3/4-oz.) can condensed cream of onion soup
1/3 cup bottled tartar sauce
1 tablespoon all-purpose flour
1/4 teaspoon dill weed
2 teaspoons lemon juice
Chopped parsley
Paprika

1. Cut 2 (12-inch-squares) of parchment paper. Butter 1 side of each parchment square; place squares buttered-side up. Place broccoli spears and pimento in 1 corner of each square. Top with fish.
2. In a medium bowl, whisk together soup, tartar sauce, flour, dill weed and lemon juice; spoon over fish. Sprinkle with parsley and paprika.
3. Fold half of each parchment square over steaks to make a triangle; fold edges together twice to seal. Place packets in a 12" x 7" baking dish. Microwave at 100% (HIGH) 6 to 8 minutes or until fish is heated through; give dish a half turn after 3 minutes. Let stand, covered, 2 minutes. Makes 2 servings.

Ginger-Lime Salmon Steaks

1/2 cup butter or margarine
1 (3" x 1-1/2") piece fresh gingerroot, peeled, cut up
2 (4- to 5-oz.) salmon steaks, about 1 inch thick
4 lime slices

1. In a food processor fitted with a steel blade, process butter or margarine and gingerroot until smooth and creamy, scraping down side of bowl often.
2. Place salmon steaks in a round, 8-inch baking dish, arranging thicker portions toward outside of dish. Spread each steak with about 1 tablespoon butter or margarine mixture. Top with lime slices. Cover with vented plastic wrap.
3. Microwave at 100% (HIGH) 3 to 4 minutes or until center of fish is beginning to flake when tested with a fork. Give dish a half turn after 2 minutes. Let stand, covered, 5 minutes.
4. Serve with lime wedges, if desired, and additional ginger-butter mixture. Cover and refrigerate any remaining ginger-butter mixture. Makes 2 servings.

How to Make Fish Fillets Amandine

1/Spread fillets with herb butter; top with parsley. Sprinkle with paprika.

2/After microwaving, sprinkle fillets with toasted slivered almonds. Garnish with parsley.

Fish Fillets Amandine

2 tablespoons butter or margarine
Dash dried leaf thyme
Dash onion salt
4 (2-oz.) fish fillets, 1/4 inch thick
About 1 tablespoon chopped parsley
Paprika to taste
2 tablespoons toasted slivered almonds

To garnish:
Parsley sprigs

1. Place butter or margarine in a 2-cup bowl. Microwave at 10% (LOW) 30 seconds or until softened; stir in thyme and onion salt.
2. Place fish fillets flat in an 8-inch-square baking dish. Spread butter or margarine mixture on fillets. Sprinkle with chopped parsley and paprika. Cover with vented plastic wrap.
3. Microwave at 100% (HIGH) 3-1/2 to 4 minutes or until center of fish is beginning to flake when tested with a fork. Give dish a half turn after 2 minutes. Sprinkle with toasted almonds. Garnish with parsley before serving. Makes 2 servings.

Tips on Fish

Breaded fish can be cooked quickly and successfully in the microwave with special browning skillets. The opposite is true for batter-coated fish, which tends to get soggy when cooked in the browning skillet. Frozen fish portions and fish sticks that are breaded give particularly good results.

To test for fish doneness, use the tines of a fork to gently lift up the flesh in the center of the fish. The flesh should be beginning to flake. It will continue cooking during the standing time. Shellfish usually turns from translucent in its raw state to opaque when cooked.

Fish is easy to defrost in the microwave. Start with a 30% (MEDIUM LOW) defrosting time, then a 10% (LOW) defrosting time, plus standing time in cold water.

How to Make Hot Shrimp Luncheon Salad

1/Drizzle dressing mixture over shrimp, tomato, celery, green onion and capers. Microwave until warm.

2/Spoon hot shrimp mixture over shredded lettuce on salad plates. Sprinkle with cheese and parsley.

Hot Shrimp Luncheon Salad

2 tablespoons vegetable oil
4 teaspoons white-wine tarragon vinegar
1 teaspoon Italian salad-dressing mix
1 cup cooked, peeled shrimp
2 tablespoons chopped tomato
1 tablespoon chopped celery
1 tablespoon chopped green onion
1 teaspoon drained capers
Shredded lettuce
1/4 cup shredded Cheddar cheese (1 oz.)
1 tablespoon chopped parsley

1. In a screw-top jar, combine oil, wine vinegar and Italian dressing mix; cover and shake well.
2. In a 1-quart bowl, combine shrimp, tomato, celery, green onion and capers. Drizzle dressing over shrimp mixture; toss gently. Microwave at 30% (MEDIUM LOW) 3 to 4 minutes or until warm; toss after 1-1/2 minutes.
3. Place lettuce on salad plates. Spoon warm shrimp mixture over lettuce. Sprinkle with cheese and parsley. Makes 2 servings.

Creamy Stuffed Manicotti

Zucchini Sauce, below
1 egg
1/2 cup cream-style cottage cheese
1/2 (9-1/4-oz.) can tuna, drained, flaked
1/4 cup herb-seasoned stuffing mix
1/4 cup chopped ripe olives
2 tablespoons grated Parmesan cheese
1 tablespoon chopped parsley
1 teaspoon chopped chives
4 manicotti shells, cooked, drained

1. Prepare Zucchini Sauce. Pour half the sauce into an 8-inch-square baking dish. Set remaining sauce aside.
2. Beat egg in a medium bowl. Stir in cottage cheese, tuna, stuffing mix, olives, Parmesan cheese, parsley and 1/2 teaspoon chives; blend well.
3. Spoon about 1/2 cup mixture into each manicotti shell. Place stuffed manicotti on top of sauce in baking dish. Pour remaining sauce over stuffed manicotti, coating all pasta.
4. Cover with vented plastic wrap. Microwave at 50% (MEDIUM) 15 to 20 minutes or until heated through, giving dish a half turn after 10 minutes.
5. At the end of cooking time, stir sauce and spoon over manicotti shell. Cover and let stand 5 minutes. Garnish with remaining chives. Makes 2 servings.

Zucchini Sauce

2 tablespoons butter or margarine
1 cup coarsely chopped zucchini
1/4 cup sliced green onion
1/4 cup chopped pimento
2 tablespoons all-purpose flour
1/2 teaspoon celery salt
1/8 teaspoon black pepper
1 cup milk

1. In a deep 1-quart casserole, combine butter or margarine, zucchini and green onion. Microwave at 100% (HIGH) 3 to 5 minutes or until barely tender.
2. Stir in pimento. Blend in flour, celery salt and pepper. Microwave at 100% (HIGH) 30 seconds.
3. Whisk in milk. Microwave at 100% (HIGH) 5 minutes or until mixture thickens and bubbles, stirring 3 times. Mixture should be thick and smooth. Makes about 2 cups.

Halibut Steaks with Corn-Bread Topping

2 bacon slices
1/4 cup chopped green onions
1/2 (8-oz.) can unsweetened crushed pineapple
1 cup coarse corn-bread crumbs
1 cup fruited granola
1/4 teaspoon dried leaf thyme
2 (6-oz.) halibut steaks, 1 inch thick
1 pineapple slice, halved crosswise

1. Place bacon on a microwave rack in a round, 8-inch baking dish. Cover with white paper towels. Microwave at 100% (HIGH) 1-1/2 to 2 minutes or until crisp. Drain bacon, reserving 1 tablespoon drippings in dish. Crumble bacon; set aside.
2. Remove microwave rack from baking dish. Add green onions to reserved bacon drippings in dish; microwave at 100% (HIGH) 2 minutes or until tender.
3. Drain pineapple, reserving 1/4 cup juice. Stir bacon, crushed pineapple, corn-bread crumbs, granola and thyme into onion mixture. Add reserved pineapple juice; stir until moistened. Remove corn-bread mixture; set aside.
4. Place halibut steaks in same baking dish, arranging thickest portions toward outside of dish. Top each steak with a mound of corn-bread mixture. Cover with vented plastic wrap.
5. Microwave at 100% (HIGH) 5 to 6 minutes or until center of fish is beginning to flake when tested with a fork. Give dish a half turn after 2-1/2 minutes.
6. Top each corn-bread mound with a half slice of pineapple. Microwave, uncovered, at 100% (HIGH) 1-1/2 minutes or until heated through. Let stand, covered, 5 minutes. Makes 2 servings.

Halibut Steaks with Corn-Bread Topping

Seafood Newburg

2 tablespoons butter or margarine
2 tablespoons all-purpose flour
1/4 teaspoon celery salt
1/4 teaspoon paprika
1/8 teaspoon onion powder
1/8 teaspoon white pepper
Dash garlic powder
1-1/2 cups half and half
1 cup cooked lump crabmeat, lobster, scallops or
   shrimp
2 tablespoons dry sherry
2 baked patty shells

1. Place butter or margarine in a deep 1-quart casserole with lid. Microwave at 100% (HIGH) 30 seconds or until melted. Stir in flour, celery salt, paprika, onion powder, white pepper and garlic powder. Microwave at 100% (HIGH) 30 seconds.
2. Whisk in half and half. Microwave at 100% (HIGH) 3-1/2 to 4-1/2 minutes or until thickened and bubbly; stir every 1 minute. Mixture should be thick and smooth.
3. Stir in seafood and sherry; blend well. Cover and microwave at 100% (HIGH) 1-1/2 to 2 minutes or until heated through; stir once. Serve in patty shells. Makes 2 servings.

Seafood Cocktail Sauce

1/4 cup chili sauce
1 tablespoon prepared horseradish
1 tablespoon finely chopped onion
1 teaspoon lemon juice
1/2 teaspoon Worcestershire sauce
1/8 to 1/4 teaspoon hot-pepper sauce

1. In a medium bowl, stir together all ingredients. Cover and refrigerate until serving time. Serve with chilled seafood dishes. Makes 1/3 cup.

Saucy Tuna Pie

2 tablespoons butter or margarine
3 tablespoons chopped onion
2 tablespoons all-purpose flour
1/4 teaspoon celery salt
1/3 cup chicken broth
1/3 cup milk
1/3 cup dairy sour cream
1 (6-1/2-oz.) can tuna, drained, flaked
1-1/2 cups frozen peas and carrots, cooked, drained
1 tablespoon chopped pimento
2 servings packaged instant mashed-potato buds
1 egg yolk
1/2 cup herb-seasoned stuffing mix
Paprika to taste

1. In a deep 1-1/2-quart casserole with lid, combine butter or margarine and onion. Microwave at 100% (HIGH) 2 minutes or until tender.
2. Stir in flour and celery salt. Microwave at 100% (HIGH) 30 seconds. Whisk in broth and milk. Microwave at 100% (HIGH) 2 to 2-1/4 minutes or until thickened and bubbly; stir every 45 seconds. Mixture should be thick and smooth.
3. Place sour cream in a small bowl. Gradually stir half the hot sauce into sour cream. Stir mixture into remaining hot sauce in casserole. Fold in tuna, peas and carrots, and pimento. Cover and microwave at 100% (HIGH) 3-1/2 to 4 minutes or until heated through; stir after 2 minutes. Cover and set aside.
4. Prepare instant mashed potatoes. Beat egg yolk into potatoes; fold in stuffing mix. Spoon potato mixture into a 7-inch pie plate.
5. Using the back of a spoon, form potatoes into a crust, building up edge above rim of pie plate. Sprinkle with paprika. Spoon tuna mixture into crust. Cover with vented plastic wrap. Microwave at 100% (HIGH) 2-1/2 to 3 minutes or until heated through; give dish a half turn after 1-1/2 minutes. Let stand, covered, 5 minutes. Garnish as desired. Makes 2 servings.

How to Make Saucy Tuna Pie

1/Stir half the hot white sauce into sour cream. This warms the sour cream so it is less likely to curdle. Stir mixture into remaining sauce in casserole.

2/To make pie filling, stir chunks of tuna, cooked peas and carrots and pimento into sour-cream sauce. Cover and microwave filling until heated through.

3/Prepare instant mashed potatoes, then beat in egg yolk and fold in herb-seasoned stuffing. Use back of a spoon to form potato mixture into a crust in a pie plate.

4/Spoon warm tuna filling into potato-stuffing crust. Cover and microwave pie until heated through. Garnish as desired.

Carnival Fried Rice

5 teaspoons butter or margarine
1 egg, beaten
2 tablespoons chopped red-bell pepper
2 tablespoons chopped green onion
1/2 teaspoon finely chopped gingerroot
1/8 teaspoon garlic powder
1-1/2 cups cooked white rice
1/4 (6-oz.) pkg. frozen Chinese pea pods, thawed
1/2 (2-1/2-oz.) jar sliced mushrooms, drained
1/4 cup fresh or drained, canned bean sprouts
1 tablespoon dry sherry
1 tablespoon soy sauce

To garnish:
Parsley sprig

1. Place 2 teaspoons butter or margarine in a 1-quart casserole. Microwave at 100% (HIGH) 30 seconds or until melted. Add beaten egg. Cover completely with plastic wrap; do not vent. Microwave at 100% (HIGH) 1 to 1-1/4 minutes or until egg is set. Let stand, covered, 5 minutes. Cut egg into strips; set aside.
2. Place 3 teaspoons butter or margarine, red pepper, green onion, gingerroot and garlic powder in 1-quart casserole. Microwave at 100% (HIGH) 2 to 2-1/2 minutes or until onion is tender. Stir in egg strips, rice, pea pods, mushrooms and bean sprouts. Toss until mixed well.
3. Stir in sherry and soy sauce. Cover and microwave at 100% (HIGH) 4 to 4-1/2 minutes or until heated through; stir after 2 minutes. Garnish with parsley. Serve with additional soy sauce, if desired. Makes 2 servings.

Oriental Vegetable Marinade

2 tablespoons vegetable oil
2 tablespoons chopped green-bell pepper
1 tablespoon chopped green onion
1 teaspoon chopped fresh gingerroot
2 tablespoons white-wine vinegar
1 tablespoon soy sauce
1/2 teaspoon sugar
1/4 teaspoon dry mustard
Dash garlic powder
2 cups any combination of Chinese pea pods, cauliflowerets, zucchini sticks
2 tablespoons radish slices

To garnish:
Toasted sesame seeds, if desired

1. In a deep 1-quart casserole, combine oil, green pepper, green onion and gingerroot. Microwave at 100% (HIGH) 1-1/2 minutes or until vegetables are crisp-tender.
2. Whisk in vinegar, soy sauce, sugar, dry mustard and garlic powder. Microwave at 100% (HIGH) 30 seconds or until boiling.
3. Add vegetables; toss until well coated. Microwave at 100% (HIGH) 1-1/2 minutes or until warm. Cover and refrigerate 3 to 4 hours; stir after 1-1/2 hours. Stir in radishes just before serving. Sprinkle with toasted sesame seeds, if desired. Makes 2 servings.

Carnival Fried Rice

Fresh Asparagus

1 lb. fresh asparagus spears
1/4 cup water

1. Wash asparagus. Grasp stalk at either end and bend in a bow shape. Stalk will break where tender part of stalk starts. Discard tough part of stalk.
2. Place spears in a flat 1-quart casserole. Add water. Cover with waxed paper or plastic wrap. Microwave at 100% (HIGH) 7 minutes or until tender; rearrange spears after 3 minutes. Let stand, covered, 2 minutes. Drain. Makes 2 servings.

Fresh Broccoli

1 lb. fresh broccoli
1/4 cup water

1. Wash broccoli; cut into flowerets leaving 2 inches of stalk. Place in a round, 8-inch baking dish, with stems toward outside of dish. Add water.
2. Cover with lid or vented plastic wrap. Microwave at 100% (HIGH) 7 to 8 minutes or until tender; rearrange spears after 3 minutes. Let stand, covered, 2 minutes. Drain. Makes 2 servings.

Frozen Peas

1 (8- to 10-oz) pkg. frozen green peas (2 cups)
1/3 cup water

1. In a 1-1/2-quart casserole with lid, combine peas and water. Cover and microwave at 100% (HIGH) 7 to 9 minutes or until tender; stir after 3 minutes. Let stand, covered, 1 to 2 minutes. Drain. Makes 2 servings.

Sliced Fresh Zucchini

2 small or 1 medium zucchini
1/4 cup water

1. Wash zucchini. Cut in 1/4-inch slices. In a 1-1/2-quart casserole with lid, combine zucchini and water. Cover and microwave at 100% (HIGH) 4 to 5 minutes or until tender; stir after 2 minutes. Drain. Makes 2 servings.

Fresh Cabbage Wedges

8 oz. (1/4 head) fresh cabbage
2 tablespoons water

1. Cut cabbage in 3 to 4 wedges. Remove outer leaves and core. In a 2-cup casserole, place wedges with core end to inside of dish. Add water. Cover with lid or plastic wrap.
2. Microwave at 100% (HIGH) 5 to 6 minutes or until tender; turn wedges over and rearrange after 3 minutes. Let stand, covered, 2 minutes. Drain. Makes 2 servings.

Fresh Artichokes

2 (10- to 12-oz.) fresh artichokes
1 tablespoon lemon juice

1. Wash artichokes under cold water. Cut off stem and 1 inch from top of each artichoke. With scissors, snip off tips of leaves. Brush cut edges with lemon juice to prevent darkening.
2. Place artichokes, stem-end down, in a deep 1-1/2-quart casserole dish. Cover with lid or vented plastic wrap. Or wrap each artichoke in waxed paper, twisting ends to seal.
3. Microwave at 100% (HIGH) 7 minutes; rearrange artichokes or give baking dish a half turn after 3 minutes. Artichokes are done when a leaf pulls out easily. Let stand, covered, 2 minutes. Serve hot with butter sauce or chill and serve with vinaigrette dressing. Makes 2 servings.

How to Cook Fresh Artichokes

1/Using a large sharp knife, cut off stem and 1 inch from pointed top of each artichoke. With scissors, snip off prickly tip of each leaf.

2/Brush cut edges of each leaf with lemon juice to prevent darkening. Wrap each artichoke in a square of waxed paper; twist ends to seal.

3/After cooking, use a grapefruit spoon to remove fuzzy center of artichoke. Leaves on the artichoke at left have been folded back to show the choke. In the foreground, notice the choke attached to the artichoke bottom or heart.

4/To eat the artichoke, remove the leaves and dip meaty end in butter sauce. Then pull the leaf through your teeth. After removing all the leaves, cut the round, cup-shaped bottom from the artichoke. Dip in butter sauce and enjoy!

How to Make Honey-Glazed Carrots

1/Peel carrots and cut into 1/2-inch pieces. A waffle cutter gives carrot slices a fancy look with little effort!

2/Cook carrots until crisp-tender. Drizzle carrots with honey.

Whole Acorn Squash

1 (1-1/4-lb.) fresh acorn squash

1. Place whole squash in microwave oven. Microwave at 100% (HIGH) 2 minutes. Pierce skin deeply several times with a large fork.
2. Microwave at 100% (HIGH) 5 to 6 minutes or until tender; turn squash over after 3 minutes. Wrap in foil and let stand 5 minutes. Cut in halves or rings. Remove seeds and membranes. Makes 2 servings.

Honey-Glazed Carrots

1-1/2 cups sliced carrots (1/2 inch thick)
1/4 cup water
2 teaspoons butter or margarine
Dash ground cinnamon
2 teaspoons honey
1 tablespoon chopped pecans

1. Wash, trim and peel carrots. In a 1-quart casserole with lid, combine carrots and water. Cover and microwave at 100% (HIGH) 8 to 9 minutes or until crisp-tender; stir after 4 minutes. Let stand, covered, 2 minutes.
2. Drain carrots and return to casserole. Stir in butter or margarine and cinnamon. Drizzle with honey; mix gently. Cover and microwave at 100% (HIGH) 30 seconds. Sprinkle with pecans. Makes 2 servings.

How to Cook Fresh Corn on the Cob

1/Here are two good ways to cook fresh corn on the cob—either in the husk or out. If you wish to husk the corn, brush ears with butter, but do not salt. Wrap ears in squares of waxed paper, twisting ends to seal.

2/To cook corn in husks, strip husks down the cob. Be careful to leave husks attached at bottom of cob. Remove corn silks. Brush ears with butter but do not salt. Pull husks back up over corn.

Fresh Corn on the Cob

2 ears fresh corn on the cob
Melted butter or margarine, if desired

To cook in waxed paper:

1. Cut squares of waxed paper. Husk corn and remove silks. Wash corn. Roll each ear with water that clings to kernels in waxed paper. Brush with melted butter or margarine before rolling up in waxed paper, if desired.
2. Twist ends of waxed paper to seal. Place in microwave oven. Microwave at 100% (HIGH) 5 minutes or until kernels are tender; rearrange ears after 2 to 3 minutes. Makes 2 servings.

To cook in the husks:
1. Carefully pull husks down ear far enough to remove silks but still keep husks attached. Brush corn with melted butter or margarine, if desired. Pull husks back over corn.
2. Quickly run husks under cold water to add moisture for cooking. Place in microwave oven. Microwave at 100% (HIGH) 5 minutes or until kernels are tender; rearrange ears after 2 to 3 minutes. Makes 2 servings.

Fresh Quartered Parsnips

2 medium, fresh parsnips
1/2 cup orange juice
2 teaspoons all-purpose flour

1. Wash, trim and peel parsnips. Cut into quarters. In a 2-quart casserole with lid, combine parsnips and 1/4 cup orange juice. Cover and microwave at 100% (HIGH) 5 to 6 minutes or until tender; stir after 3 minutes.
2. In a screw-top jar, shake together flour and 1/4 cup orange juice; stir into parsnips and juices. Cover and microwave at 100% (HIGH) 2-1/2 minutes or until thickened and bubbly; stir after 1-1/2 minutes. Let stand, covered, 2 minutes. Makes 2 servings.

How to Make Dill-Buttered New Potatoes

1/Peel a small strip of skin around center of each tiny red potato to prevent skins from breaking during cooking.

2/Hot water gives potatoes a faster start in microwave cooking. Drain potatoes and toss with butter and dill weed.

Twice-Baked Sweet Potatoes

2 sweet potatoes or yams
6 tablespoons caramel or butterscotch ice-cream
  topping
2 tablespoons butter or margarine
1/8 teaspoon ground cinnamon
Dash ground nutmeg
2 teaspoons toasted chopped pecans, if desired

1. Wash potatoes. Pierce each potato several times with a large fork to allow steam to escape. Place potatoes in microwave oven. Microwave at 100% (HIGH) 6 to 7 minutes; turn potatoes over and rearrange after 3 minutes. When done, potatoes should be almost tender in center when pierced with a fork. Wrap in foil. Let stand 5 minutes.
2. Cut top off hot baked potatoes. Quickly scoop out hot potato pulp with a spoon, being careful to keep shells intact. Set shells aside.
3. In a mixing bowl, combine hot potato pulp, 1/4 cup ice-cream topping, butter or margarine, cinnamon and nutmeg. Beat with electric mixer on high speed until fluffy. Spoon mixture into potato shells. Place on a serving plate.
4. Cover with vented plastic wrap. Microwave at 100% (HIGH) 3 to 4 minutes or until heated through. Top with remaining 2 tablespoons topping; sprinkle with chopped pecans, if desired. Makes 2 servings.

Dill-Buttered New Potatoes

1 lb. tiny new potatoes (about 7)
2-1/2 cups hot water
2 tablespoons butter or margarine
1/2 teaspoon dill weed

1. Wash potatoes. Halve any large potatoes so all potatoes are about the same size. Peel off a small strip of skin around center of whole potatoes.
2. In a deep 2-quart casserole with lid, combine potatoes and hot water to cover. Cover and microwave at 100% (HIGH) 15 to 17 minutes or until potatoes are fork-tender; stir after 8 minutes. Let stand, covered, 2 minutes. Drain. Add butter or margarine and dill weed; toss until all potatoes are well coated. Makes 2 servings.

Twice-Baked Sweet Potatoes

Vegetable Garnish Ideas

1/Try simple toppings such as crumbled bacon, flavored croutons, toasted nuts or seeds, or shredded cheeses on plain vegetables. Fresh herbs, buttered cracker crumbs or canned French-fried onions turn everyday vegetables into something special.

2/Top hot cooked vegetables with yogurt, sour-cream dip, cheese or hollandaise sauce. Snip fresh chives over the topping.

Tomato Stars

2 large tomatoes
Celery salt to taste
1/4 cup grated Parmesan cheese (1 oz.)
1/4 cup mayonnaise or salad dressing
1/2 (8-oz.) can artichokes, drained, chopped
1 tablespoon chopped watercress
1 teaspoon drained capers

To garnish:
Capers
Paprika, if desired

1. Place uncored tomatoes, stem-end down, on a cutting board. Cut in 6 to 8 wedges, cutting to but not through bottom of tomato to form stars.
2. Place tomatoes in a 10" x 6" baking dish. Sprinkle inside of tomatoes with celery salt; set aside.
3. In a medium bowl, stir together Parmesan cheese, mayonnaise or salad dressing, artichokes, watercress and capers. Spoon artichoke mixture into tomatoes, using about 1/3 cup for each. Cover with vented plastic wrap.
4. Microwave at 100% (HIGH) 3 to 4 minutes or until warmed through; give dish a half turn after 2 minutes. Let stand, covered, 2 minutes. Garnish with additional capers and paprika, if desired. Makes 2 servings.

Tips on Vegetables

Vegetables cooked in the microwave have more flavor because they cook quickly. They usually require little or no water that might dilute some of the flavor. Studies indicate that vegetables cooked in the microwave actually retain more of their nutrients.

Cooking times are generally given for crisp-tender vegetables. When pierced with a fork, crisp-tender vegetables will still have a little resistance. Vegetables continue to cook during the standing time, so allow for that when estimating doneness. If you prefer well-done vegetables, add cooking time in 30- to 60-second amounts. Baked potatoes should be cooked until still slightly firm, then wrapped in foil for the standing time to finish cooking. Potatoes cooked until tender to the touch will be shriveled by the time they are served.

Vegetables are stirred during cooking so they will cook more evenly. If they are not moved around, the vegetables close to the edges of the dish will overcook before the vegetables in the center are done. To rearrange vegetables in a pouch, pick up the pouch and flex it several times to move the frozen vegetables in the center toward the outside of the pouch. In the case of larger vegetables that cannot be stirred, move the center pieces to the outside of the dish and the pieces from the outside to the center.

Tomato Stars

Herbed Vegetable Marinade

2 tablespoons tarragon wine vinegar
2 tablespoons lemon juice
1 small garlic clove, minced
1/4 teaspoon dried leaf basil
1/4 teaspoon fennel seed
1/8 teaspoon celery salt
1/8 teaspoon coarsely ground pepper
1/4 cup vegetable oil
2 cups any combination of sliced mushrooms, onion rings, halved cherry tomatoes, halved canned artichoke hearts
2 tablespoons chopped parsley

---

1. In a deep 1-quart casserole with lid, combine vinegar, lemon juice, garlic, basil, fennel seed, celery salt and pepper. Gradually whisk in oil. Microwave at 100% (HIGH) 45 to 60 seconds or until boiling.
2. Add vegetables; toss until well coated. Microwave at 100% (HIGH) 1 minute or until warm. Cover and refrigerate 3 to 4 hours; stir after 1-1/2 hours. Stir in parsley before serving. Makes 2 servings.

Dilled Butter Sauce

1/4 cup butter or margarine
1 tablespoon lemon juice
1/4 teaspoon dill weed
1/8 teaspoon onion powder
1/8 teaspoon celery salt
Dash white pepper

---

1. In a 2-cup bowl, melt butter or margarine at 100% (HIGH) 45 seconds. Stir in lemon juice, dill weed, onion powder, celery salt and white pepper. Serve warm as an artichoke dipper or with other vegetables. Makes 2 servings.

Marinated Vegetable Kabobs

1/4 medium green-bell pepper, cut in wedges
1/4 medium red-bell pepper, cut in wedges
1/2 small onion, cut in wedges
3 tablespoons water
1/2 cup oil-base salad dressing with herbs and spices
2 tablespoons dry white wine
2 teaspoons Worcestershire sauce
1/4 teaspoon dried leaf tarragon
4 fresh mushrooms
1/2 (14-1/2-oz.) can artichoke hearts, drained
4 cherry tomatoes

---

1. In a medium bowl, combine green and red peppers, onion and water. Cover with waxed paper or plastic wrap. Microwave at 100% (HIGH) 3 minutes or until crisp-tender. Remove vegetables with a slotted spoon, reserving juices in bowl. Set vegetables aside.
2. To vegetable juice in bowl, add salad dressing, wine, Worcestershire sauce and tarragon; whisk until combined. Microwave at 100% (HIGH) 1-1/2 to 2 minutes or until boiling. Add pepper and onion wedges, mushrooms and artichoke hearts. Cover and marinate at room temperature 30 minutes; stir occasionally.
3. To serve, drain vegetables, reserving marinade. Thread marinated vegetables and tomatoes alternately on 12-inch bamboo skewers. Place in a 10" x 6" baking dish. Drizzle with some of the reserved marinade. Cover with vented plastic wrap. Microwave at 100% (HIGH) 3 minutes or until heated through; drizzle with reserved marinade after 2 minutes. Let stand, covered, 2 minutes. Serve over rice, if desired. Makes 2 servings.

Marinated Vegetable Kabobs

1/Cut a slice from top and bottom of each onion. This keeps inside of onions from exploding during cooking. For the same reason, pierce each onion several times with a large fork. Wrap each onion in a square of waxed paper, twisting ends to seal.

2/Let herb butter mellow at room temperature before serving over piping hot onions. These onions make a tasty and attractive garnish for a steak or roast platter.

Baked Onions with Herb Butter

1/4 cup butter or margarine
1/4 teaspoon celery salt
1/4 teaspoon parsley flakes
1/4 teaspoon dried leaf tarragon
2 medium onions

1. Place butter or margarine in a small bowl. Microwave at 10% (LOW) 30 seconds or until softened. Add celery salt, parsley and tarragon; mix well. Set butter or margarine mixture aside at room temperature.
2. Wash onions, leaving outer skin intact. Trim top and bottom off each onion. Pierce onions deeply several times with a large fork. Wrap each onion in waxed paper, twisting ends loosely to seal. Microwave at 100% (HIGH) 5 to 7 minutes or until tender; turn onions over and rearrange after 3 minutes. Let stand, wrapped, 2 minutes.
3. To serve, top onions with herb-butter mixture. Makes 2 servings.

Variation
To use large onions, prepare and wrap in waxed paper as above. Microwave onions at 100% (HIGH) 5 minutes for 1 large onion, 10 to 12 minutes for 2 large onions. Let stand, wrapped, 2 minutes. Cut onions in half to serve.

Kohlrabi Oriental-Style

1 (8-oz.) kohlrabi, peeled, thinly sliced (1-1/2 cups)
1 teaspoon finely chopped fresh gingerroot
1 tablespoon vegetable oil
1/2 (6-oz.) pkg. frozen Chinese pea pods, thawed
1/2 small red-bell pepper, cut in strips
2 tablespoons chopped onion
1 teaspoon soy sauce
1 teaspoon white vinegar

1. In a 1-quart casserole with lid, combine kohlrabi, gingerroot and oil. Cover and microwave at 100% (HIGH) 3 to 4 minutes; stir after 2 minutes.
2. Stir in pea pods, red pepper and onion. Sprinkle with soy sauce and vinegar; toss well. Cover and microwave at 100% (HIGH) 3 minutes or until vegetables are crisp-tender; stir after 2 minutes. Serve with additional soy sauce, if desired. Makes 2 servings.

How to Make Curried Broccoli Deluxe

1/In a flat baking dish or 2 small dishes, arrange cooked broccoli spears so the stalks alternate toward edge of dish. Tuck in slices of hard-cooked egg.

2/Drizzle curry sauce evenly over casserole. Microwave, then sprinkle with crumbs after heating so crumbs do not become tough.

Curried Broccoli Deluxe

1 tablespoon butter or margarine
1/4 cup seasoned dry bread crumbs
1 tablespoon chopped parsley
1 (10-oz.) pkg. frozen broccoli spears, cooked, drained
2 hard-cooked eggs, sliced
1/2 (10-1/2-oz.) can condensed cream of onion soup
2 tablespoons dry white wine
2 tablespoons mayonnaise or salad dressing
1/2 teaspoon curry powder

1. In a small bowl, microwave butter or margarine at 100% (HIGH) 30 seconds or until melted. Stir in bread crumbs and parsley; set aside.
2. In 2 small dishes, arrange broccoli spears and egg slices. In a medium bowl, whisk together onion soup, wine, mayonnaise or salad dressing and curry powder. Cover with vented plastic wrap. Microwave at 100% (HIGH) 2 minutes or until hot; stir after 1 minute.
3. Pour hot sauce over broccoli and eggs. Cover with plastic wrap. Microwave at 100% (HIGH) 3 minutes or until heated through; give dish a half turn after 1-1/2 minutes. Sprinkle with buttered bread crumbs. Makes 2 servings.

Frosted Cauliflower

1/2 head whole cauliflower
2 tablespoons water
1/4 cup sour cream and chive dip
1/4 teaspoon dry mustard
1/8 teaspoon celery seed
1/2 cup shredded Cheddar cheese (2 oz.)
Salad seasoning

1. Wash and core cauliflower, leaving head intact. Remove excess leaves. Place cauliflower, stem-end down, in a deep 1-quart casserole with lid. Add water. Cover and microwave at 100% (HIGH) 5 to 6 minutes or until tender; give dish a half turn after 3 minutes. Let stand, covered, 2 minutes. Drain.
2. In a small bowl, stir together dip, dry mustard and celery seed. Spread over hot cauliflower in casserole. Sprinkle with Cheddar cheese; then sprinkle generously with salad seasoning. Microwave, uncovered, at 100% (HIGH) 1 to 1-1/4 minutes or until cheese melts; give dish a half turn after 30 seconds. Makes 2 servings.

Desserts

Flaming Fruit Sauce

1 (10-oz.) pkg. frozen fruit in syrup, thawed
2 teaspoons cornstarch
2 teaspoons lemon juice
2 tablespoons fruit-flavored brandy or liqueur
Ice cream or sherbet

1. Drain fruit, reserving 1/3 cup syrup. In a 1-quart bowl, combine cornstarch and a little reserved syrup until smooth. Stir in remaining reserved syrup and lemon juice. Microwave at 100% (HIGH) 1-1/2 to 2 minutes until thickened and bubbly. Fold in fruit.
2. In a 1-cup glass measuring cup, heat brandy or liqueur at 100% (HIGH) 10 seconds. Pour hot brandy or liqueur into a large ladle. Carefully ignite and pour over fruits. Stir when flame subsides. Serve over ice cream or sherbet. Makes 1-1/4 cups.

Velvet Fudge Sauce

1 (6-oz.) pkg. semisweet chocolate pieces (1 cup)
1 (5-1/3-oz.) can evaporated milk (2/3 cup)
1/2 (7-oz.) jar marshmallow creme

1. In a 1-quart bowl, combine chocolate pieces and evaporated milk. Microwave at 100% (HIGH) 2 minutes or until chocolate pieces are almost melted; stir after 1 minute. Stir until smooth.
2. Add marshmallow creme in spoonfuls. Microwave at 100% (HIGH) 30 seconds or until marshmallow creme softens. Stir vigorously until blended. Serve warm. Refrigerate remaining sauce. Makes 2 cups.

Fruit-Nut Crispy Bars

2 cups crisp rice cereal
1/4 cup chopped dried apricots
1/4 cup chopped candied cherries
1/4 cup chopped nuts
2 tablespoons butter or margarine, cut up
15 large marshmallows

1. Measure cereal, apricots, cherries and nuts; set aside.
2. Butter an 8-inch-square baking dish. Place butter or margarine and marshmallows in a 2-quart bowl. Microwave at 100% (HIGH) 1 minute or until melted; stir to blend.
3. Quickly stir in cereal, fruits and nuts. With buttered fingers, press gently into buttered baking dish. Cool completely before cutting into bars. Makes 30 bars.

Applesauce

3 cups peeled, quartered cooking apples
1/4 cup apple juice
2 to 3 tablespoons sugar

1. In a deep 1-1/2-quart casserole with lid, combine apples, apple juice and sugar. Cover and microwave at 100% (HIGH) 6 to 7 minutes or until apples are tender; stir after 3 minutes.
2. Mash apples to desired consistency by hand or process in a food processor fitted with a steel blade. Makes 1-1/2 cups.

Flaming Fruit Sauce

Vanilla Pudding

1/3 cup sugar
1 tablespoon cornstarch
1 cup milk
1 egg yolk, slightly beaten
1 tablespoon butter or margarine
1/2 teaspoon vanilla extract

1. In a 1-1/2-quart bowl, combine sugar and cornstarch, mixing thoroughly; stir in milk. Microwave at 100% (HIGH) 3 to 4 minutes or until mixture is thickened and bubbly; stir every 1 minute.
2. Stir a small amount of hot mixture into beaten egg yolks; stir yolk mixture into hot mixture. Microwave at 100% (HIGH) 45 seconds or until thickened; stir every 15 seconds.
3. Stir in butter or margarine until melted. Stir in vanilla. Pour into dessert dishes and refrigerate until set. Makes 1 to 2 servings.

Variation
Chocolate Pudding: Add 1/2 cup semisweet chocolate pieces to thickened mixture before adding egg yolk. Microwave at 100% (HIGH) 30 to 45 seconds. Stir until chocolate is melted. Continue with egg yolk as above.

Cranberry Cloud Parfaits

2 teaspoons unflavored gelatin powder
1/4 cup cold water
1 cup fresh cranberries
1 egg white
1/2 cup sugar
2 teaspoons lemon juice

1. In a small bowl, soften gelatin in cold water 5 minutes. In a deep 1-quart casserole, combine cranberries and gelatin mixture. Microwave at 100% (HIGH) 2 minutes or until boiling; stir well. Microwave at 30% (MEDIUM LOW) 3 minutes or until cranberry skins pop; stir after 1-1/2 minutes. Cool to room temperature.
2. In a medium bowl, combine egg white, sugar, lemon juice and cranberry mixture. Beat with electric mixer at high speed 8 to 10 minutes or until mixture forms soft peaks. Gently pile into 6-ounce parfait glasses. Refrigerate. Makes 2 servings.

Strawberry Banana Splits

1 tablespoon butter or margarine
1/4 cup strawberry ice-cream topping
1 tablespoon banana liqueur or strawberry liqueur
2 tablespoons chopped nuts
2 bananas, halved lengthwise and crosswise
1/2 pint strawberry ice cream

To garnish:
Fresh strawberries
Whipped cream

1. Place butter or margarine in a round, 8-inch baking dish. Microwave at 100% (HIGH) 30 seconds or until melted. Stir in strawberry topping, liqueur and nuts. Add bananas, turning gently to coat with sauce. Cover with vented plastic wrap.
2. Microwave at 100% (HIGH) 1 to 2 minutes or until bananas are warmed through; rearrange once. Spoon bananas into serving dishes. Top with scoops of ice cream. Drizzle with warm strawberry sauce from baking dish. Garnish with fresh strawberries and whipped cream. Makes 2 servings.

Fruit Crisp

Apple Crisp Topping, opposite
1 (21-oz.) can fruit-pie filling
1 tablespoon lemon juice
Cream or vanilla ice cream

1. Prepare topping mixture; set aside.
2. Combine pie filling and lemon juice in a 9-inch pie plate. Sprinkle with topping mixture. Microwave, uncovered, at 100% (HIGH) 8 to 10 minutes or until mixture is bubbling around edges; give dish a half turn after 4 minutes. Serve warm with cream or vanilla ice cream. Makes 2 large servings.

How to Make Apple Crisp

1/Thoroughly mix granulated sugar, brown sugar, flour, oats and spices for topping. Use a pastry blender or 2 knives to cut in butter until mixture resembles coarse crumbs.

2/Here's an easy way to slice apples. Cut apple in 4 large pieces leaving the square core in the center. Turn each apple piece flat side down and slice to desired thickness.

3/Place sliced apples in baking dish, then drizzle with apple juice. Sprinkle topping evenly over apples.

4/Serve warm crisp in sherbet dishes with generous scoops of vanilla ice cream or cinnamon ice cream.

Apple Crisp

3 cups peeled, sliced cooking apples
2 tablespoons apple juice

Topping:
1/4 cup granulated sugar
1/4 cup packed brown sugar
1/4 cup all-purpose flour
1/4 cup quick-cooking rolled oats
1/2 teaspoon ground cinnamon
1/4 teaspoon ground nutmeg
2 tablespoons butter or margarine

1. Prepare topping mixture. Butter a 7-inch pie plate. Place apples in baking dish. Drizzle with apple juice. Sprinkle with topping mixture. Microwave, uncovered, at 100% (HIGH) 7 to 8 minutes or until apples are tender; give dish a half turn after 4 minutes.
2. Serve warm with cream or vanilla or cinnamon ice cream, if desired. Makes 2 servings.
Topping:
1. In a medium bowl, combine granulated sugar, brown sugar, flour, oats, cinnamon and nutmeg. Cut in butter or margarine until mixture resembles coarse crumbs.

Baked Pears

2 (7-oz.) firm, ripe pears
2 tablespoons raisins
2 tablespoons brown sugar
Ground cinnamon
Ground nutmeg
1/4 cup bourbon or apple juice.
Vanilla ice cream or cream

1. Core pears, being careful not to cut through bottoms. Peel a small strip around top of each pear. Set pears, stem-side up, in a 9" x 5" loaf dish.
2. Spoon raisins into center of each pear. Mound brown sugar on pears. Sprinkle with cinnamon and nutmeg. Drizzle with bourbon or apple juice. Cover with vented plastic wrap.
3. Microwave at 100% (HIGH) 5 to 6 minutes or until almost tender; give dish a half turn after 3 minutes. Let stand, covered, 10 minutes. Spoon pan juices over apples. Serve with ice cream or cream and additional cinnamon, if desired. Makes 2 servings.

Old-Fashioned Custard

2/3 cup milk
1 egg
4 teaspoons sugar
1/2 teaspoon vanilla extract
Ground nutmeg to taste

1. In a 1-cup glass measuring cup, microwave milk at 100% (HIGH) 1-1/2 to 2 minutes or until very hot but not boiling. In a medium bowl, whisk together egg, sugar and vanilla. Gradually stir in hot milk.
2. Divide egg mixture between 2 (6-ounce) custard cups. Sprinkle with nutmeg. Pour hot water into a 9" x 5" loaf dish to a depth of 3/4 inch. Set custard cups in baking dish. Water should be 1 inch deep around cups.
3. Microwave at 100% (HIGH) 3-1/2 to 4-1/2 minutes or until custard is nearly set but still moves slightly in center. Give baking dish a half turn and individual custards a half turn after 2 minutes. Check custards at minimum time and remove any that are done. Continue cooking remaining custards. Cool on a rack only until set; then serve or refrigerate. May be served warm or chilled. Makes 2 servings.

Variation

Crème Brûlée: Sieve a generous coating of brown sugar over refrigerated custard. Set custards in a baking pan. Pack crushed ice around custard dishes. Broil in preheated conventional oven 5 inches from heat 3 minutes or until brown sugar is melted.

Make-Ahead Granola-Applesauce Muffins

2 teaspoons lemon juice
3/4 cup milk
1/2 cup water
1-1/2 cups granola with fruits and nuts
1/2 cup applesauce
1/4 cup vegetable oil
1 egg, beaten
1-1/4 cups all-purpose flour
1/2 cup sugar
1 teaspoon baking powder
1 teaspoon baking soda
1/2 teaspoon salt
1 teaspoon ground cinnamon
1/2 teaspoon ground nutmeg

1. Stir lemon juice into milk; set aside.
2. Place water in a 2-quart bowl. Microwave at 100% (HIGH) 1-1/2 to 2 minutes or until boiling. Sprinkle granola into boiling water; stir until moistened. Stir in milk mixture, applesauce, oil and eggs; mix well.
3. In a medium bowl, stir together flour, sugar, baking powder, baking soda, salt, cinnamon and nutmeg. Add flour mixture to granola mixture; stir until moistened.
4. Cover and refrigerate batter up to 3 weeks.
5. **To microwave muffins:** Spoon 2 tablespoons granola batter into paper baking cups placed in a microwave muffin pan or in 5-ounce custard cups. Arrange custard cups in a ring in the microwave oven.
6. Microwave at 100% (HIGH) for time in chart below or until a wooden pick inserted in center comes out clean. Cool on a rack. If desired, brush warm muffins with melted butter or margarine and sprinkle with a mixture of cinnamon, sugar and grated orange peel. Makes 30 muffins.

SERVINGS	4 muffins	2 muffins	1 muffin
Time at HIGH	1 minute, 40 seconds	55 seconds	40 seconds

Dried Mixed Fruit

1/2 (8-oz.) pkg. dried mixed fruit (1 cup)
About 1 cup hot water
2 tablespoons sugar

1. Place fruit in a deep 1-quart casserole with lid. Add hot water to cover fruit. Cover and microwave at 100% (HIGH) 3 to 4 minutes or until boiling. Stir and cover.
2. Microwave at 30% (MEDIUM LOW) 9 to 10 minutes or until nearly tender. Stir in sugar. Cover and microwave at 30% (MEDIUM LOW) 2 minutes or until sugar dissolves. Makes 2 servings.

How to Make Granola-Applesauce Muffins

1/Sprinkle granola into boiling water, then stir until moistened. Stir in remaining ingredients. Cover and refrigerate up to 3 weeks.

2/To bake muffins, spoon 2 tablespoons batter into each paper baking cup set in custard cups or a microwave muffin pan. Cups should be only half full.

3/Microwave muffins at 100% (HIGH). To test muffins for doneness, a wooden pick inserted in center should come out clean, not with batter clinging to it as shown.

4/To serve, brush warm muffins with melted butter or margarine, then sprinkle with a mixture of sugar, ground cinnamon and grated orange peel.

Index